Real Sofistikashun

Also by Tony Hoagland

POETRY

Sweet Ruin
Donkey Gospel
What Narcissism Means to Me
Unincorporated Persons in the Late Honda Dynasty
Application for Release from the Dream
Recent Changes in the Vernacular
Priest Turned Therapist Treats Fear of God

ESSAYS

Twenty Poems That Could Save America and Other Essays
The Art of Voice: Poetic Principles and Practice
(with Kay Cosgrove)
The Underground Poetry Metro Transportation System for Souls:
Essays on the Cultural Life of Poetry

TRANSLATION

Cinderbiter: Celtic Poems (versions with Martin Shaw)

Real Sofistikashun

ESSAYS ON POETRY AND CRAFT

Tony Hoagland

Graywolf Press

Publication of this volume is made possible in part by a grant provided by the Minnesota State Arts Board, through an appropriation by the Minnesota State Legislature; a grant from the Wells Fargo Foundation Minnesota; and a grant from the National Endowment for the Arts, which believes that a great nation deserves great art. Significant support has also been provided by the Bush Foundation; Target; the McKnight Foundation; and other generous contributions from foundations, corporations, and individuals. To these organizations and individuals we offer our heartfelt thanks.

Published by Graywolf Press
250 Third Avenue North, Suite 600
Minneapolis, Minnesota 55401

www.graywolfpress.org

Published in the United States of America

ISBN 978-1-55597-455-8

  8 10 12 13 11 9 7

Library of Congress Control Number: 2006924335

Cover design: Jeenee Lee

Cover art: Detail of a painting of Shiva riding on a parrot. Punjab Hills, Kangra style. Circa 1820 AD
© Copyright the Trustees of the British Museum

Acknowledgments

Thanks to the editors of the periodicals in which some of these essays were first published, in different versions:

The American Poetry Review: "Negative Capability: How to Talk Mean and Influence People"; "Three Tenors: Pinsky, Hass, Glück, and the Deployment of Talent"
The Cortland Review: "Fragment, Juxtaposition, and Completeness: Some Notes and Preferences"
Parnassus: "On Disproportion"
Poetry: "Fear of Narrative and the Skittery Poem of Our Moment"
Southern Indiana Review: "Altitudes, a Homemade Taxonomy: Image, Diction, and Rhetoric"
The Writer's Chronicle: "'Tis Backed like a Weasel': The Slipperiness of Metaphor"; "Two Roads Diverged: Character, Metaphor, and Destiny in the Poems of Matthews and Levis"; "Sad Anthropologists: The Dialectical Use of Tone"; "Thingitude and Causality: In Praise of Materialism"; "Self-Consciousness"

"On Disproportion" was reprinted in the anthology *Poets Teaching Poets: Self and the World,* Gregory Orr and Ellen Bryant Voigt, editors (University of Michigan Press, 1996).
"'Tis Backed Like a Weasel': The Slipperiness of Metaphor" was reprinted in *Poet's Work, Poet's Play,* Daniel Tobin and Pimone Triplett, editors (University of Michigan Press).

These essays have been a long time in their writing and revision, and there are many persons to whom I owe a debt for their help and encouragement: Chris Matthews, Ken Hart, Kathleen Lee, Carl Dennis, Steve Orlen, Ellen Bryant Voigt, Michael Bowden, Betty Sasaki, Peter Harris, David Rivard, Dean Young, Peter Turchi, Eleanor Wilner, Catherine Barnett, Adrian Blevins, Marie Howe, Jason Shinder, Kevin McIlvoy, and Terrance Hayes. Special thanks to Anne, Fiona, and Jeff.

Thanks, too, to the Guggenheim Foundation, the University of Pittsburgh, and the University of Houston for their support.

Most especially I have to thank my colleagues and students in the Warren Wilson College MFA program, that rare forum, which gave me my first place in an intellectual community.

Grateful acknowledgment is made to the following for permission to reprint previously published material:

"Ocean-Letter" and "Monday in Christine Street" from *Calligrammes* by Guillaume Apollinaire, © 2004 The Regents of the University of California, University of California Press.

"#9" from *Plantain:* "Twenty-first. Night. Monday" from *Twenty Poems of Anna Akhmatova*, translated from the Russian by Jane Kenyon with Vera Sandomirsky Dunham, in *Collected Poems of Jane Kenyon*, copyright © 2005, reprinted by permission of Graywolf Press.

"Mommy Is a Scary Narcissist" from *Allegory of the Supermarket* by Stephanie Brown. Copyright © 1999 by Stephanie Brown. Reprinted by permission of the University of Georgia Press.

"Man in Space" is from *The Art of Drowning*, by Billy Collins, © 1995. Reprinted by permission of the University of Pittsburgh Press.

"On Earth" from *Blue Hour* by Carolyn Forché. Copyright © 2003 by Carolyn Forché. Reprinted by permission of HarperCollins Publishers.

"Last Breath in Snowfall" from *Deposition*. Copyright © 2002 by Katie Ford. Reprinted by permission of Graywolf Press.

"Married," copyright © 1994 by Jack Gilbert, from *The Great Fires: Poems 1982–1992* by Jack Gilbert. Used by permission of Alfred A. Knopf, a division of Random House, Inc.

"Love Poem" from *The First Four Books of Poems* by Louise Glück. Copyright © 1968, 1971, 1972, 1973, 1974, 1975, 1976, 1977, 1978, 1979, 1980, 1985, 1995 by Louise Glück. Reprinted by permission of HarperCollins Publishers. "Purple Bathing Suit" is from *Meadowlands*. Copyright © 1997 by Louise Glück. Reprinted by permission of HarperCollins Publishers.

Contents

for Carl Dennis

Foreword

My friend Paul once said to me, "Scholars *look* things up; poets *make* things up." Though I would not justify ignorance in such a blithe, prideful way, there's something true and Emersonian about what he says, about finding out for yourself. This collection of essays about poetry, neither academic nor exactly for the reader off the street, is in fact a mostly homemade set of geographies, jerry-rigged descriptions, and taxonomies. They are intended for the reader who loves poems and likes to think about them. My hope is that these pieces show one person trying to think through certain topics, and that the step-by-step process of that thinking will be helpful to both readers and writers—in part because the essays *are* rudimentary, feeling their way. It's not the spirit of ignorance I feel loyal to, but the spirit of amateurism.

No program or prescription for American poetry is being argued here. Nevertheless, there are underlying orientations and affections. If a vision of poetry comes through, I expect it reflects an allegiance to experience as much as to art; a love for the sinuous human voice, for elaborate sentences, and for a certain brashness of imagination.

T.H.

Altitudes, a Homemade Taxonomy

IMAGE, DICTION, AND RHETORIC

In the Indian system of kundalini yoga, the human body possesses seven energy centers, called chakras. These energy points are arranged in a vertical line from the lower tip of the spine to the top of the skull: genitals, belly, heart, throat, third eye, etc. The seven chakras are variously equated with sexuality, power, compassion, and insight. Yoga exercises are intended to open and develop these aspects of human potential. Without stretching the analogy too far, in this essay I would like to use that image to suggest that there are poetic chakras, too—centers of power to which a particular poet may be attuned, from which she or he may exercise certain poetic powers. As the chakras are located at specific places in the body, so certain poetic strengths might be aligned with specific poetic devices, distinct capabilities of the language.

Any serious student of art eventually begins to make such discriminations. In comparing differences of aesthetic temperament, we observe that one artist is passionate, raw, visceral, working from the unconscious, the id; another is cerebral, cool, and refined. Jackson

1

Pollock is hot and raw, Mark Rothko is spiritual and moody, Paul Klee is witty and slim and whimsical. I often ask a group of students, at the beginning of a workshop, to describe their work in terms of its most characteristic emotion, or "humour"—whether they write from a taproot of rage, pity, love, or grief. It seems as important to know this about yourself as to know your country of origin. Do you come from the earthy erotic Mediterranean, or from the snowy discriminating Nordic cerebral cortex? Are you a Kazantzakis or a Tranströmer? People cry from their guts; they makes jokes with their heads and mouths. James Wright sobs, "I wouldn't / lie to you." Robert Hass *discerns*: "Longing, we say because desire is full of endless distances." Hass speaks from higher in the body than Wright.

But you see how quickly the spatial metaphors, especially of altitude, with their accompanying implications of relative value, creep in. The superego is "higher" than the id; thinking is "higher" than feeling; the heart is higher than the genitals. But despite this governing metaphor of altitude, a taxonomy of poetic chakras has little to do with valuations of better and lesser.

What can be said with some certainty is that various aspects of poetry are *exerted* from different centers of power in the self. These centers represent distinct capacities of human consciousness. And these poetic chakras elicit response from different altitudes in the reader. The three centers of power I want to identify here are image, diction, and rhetoric. Images could be said to embody the intuitive and unmediated knowledge of the unconscious. Diction, with its powers of inflection, is especially useful for expressing intellectual discriminations. Rhetoric is the willful shaping of attitude in a poem.

Of course this is only a system, a typology. The powers of language are never perfectly discrete. Good poems are fusions and interplay, ever shifting between and collaging the various powers. However, to break them into categories is a useful way of seeing more clearly what they are.

Image

Nothing is more potent in poetry than image; its power is the appeal of unmediated communication. On the scale of immediate gratification, image scores high. Many poets and many readers remain centered in the image chakra all their lives, with no complaint, and not from being simpleminded, either. The ability of images to carry complex information is tremendous. Consider this poem by Sharon Olds, a poet noted for the power of her image-making.

My Son the Man

> Suddenly his shoulders get a lot wider,
> the way Houdini would expand his body
> while people were putting him in chains. It seems
> no time since I would help him put on his sleeper,
> guide his calves into the shadowy interior,
> zip him up and toss him up and
> catch his weight. I cannot imagine him
> no longer a child, and I know I must get ready,
> get over my fear of men now my son
> is going to be one. This was not
> what I had in mind when he pressed up through me like a
> sealed trunk through the ice of the Hudson,
> snapped the padlock, unsnaked the chains,
> appeared in my arms. No he looks at me
> the way Houdini studied a box
> to learn the way out, then smiled and let himself be manacled.

Where do images, which do most of the important work in this poem, come from? Is it merely genius that makes Olds such a strong poet? Of course, her imagery is brilliant, we all have encountered wonderful image-makers who never come close to Olds's accomplishment. Resourceful as the images are in "My Son the Man," they would count for little unless the poet had crafted them into an effective drama, a narrative of their own. If we study the poem a little, we see that the speaker's description of her son, expressed in terms of the Houdini story, is dense with images of confinement (the sleeper, chains, sealed trunk, and box). The dramatic peak of the poem is the moment of reversal, which transposes the speaker from her position of being the careful observer of her son into the one being observed; moreover, and dramatically, she finds herself perceived as a prison to be escaped from.

It is the speed and simultaneity of the metaphorical process, the nonverbal transformations of image, its embodiedness, which partially account for the excitement of reading the poem. But it's also the elusive, multiple resonances concealed in such subterranean systems. For example, the way a shift in ego-power is indicated by the son's confident smile. Standing farther back from the poem, we can see that it is rife with images of known and unknown—under and above, inside and out. That the "trunk" which appears as a birth image is "sealed" suggests the speaker's impending surprise at what she has received. The particular resonances might be explicated but can't be ascribed to calculation or mere intelligence. The fact that the narrator does not overtly interpret or explain is significant. Olds's trust in the discoveries of image allows the poem its strength.

The manufacture of images is often attributed to the unconscious. Though some images are more self-conscious than others, this poem by Olds seems a good example of poetic power exerted from the gut, or at least someplace other than the head. Is it the heart? The uterus? It would be inaccurate to call the power here *primitive*, but it is visceral. It has a potency that does not require a lot of explication.

We can see the same deep psychic intelligence, mediated and delivered by image, in the poem "Tu Do Street" by Yusef Komunyakaa. This poem draws from the poet's Vietnam war experience and abundantly employs both literal and figurative images:

> Music divides the evening.
> I close my eyes & can see
> men drawing lines in the dust.
> America pushes through the membrane
> of mist & smoke, & I'm a small boy
> again in Bogalusa: *White Only*
> signs and Hank Snow. But tonight
> I walk into a place where bar girls
> fade like tropical birds.
> . . . .
> Back in the bush at Dak To
> & Khe Sanh, we fought
> the brothers of these women
> we now run to hold in our arms.

> There's more than a nation
> inside us, as black & white
> soldiers touch the same lovers
> minutes apart, tasting
> each other's breath,
> without knowing these rooms
> run into each other like tunnels
> leading to the underworld.

Komunyaka's style itself is largely imagistic, a lyrical narrative delivered in sequences of images, layering the worlds of past and present, childhood and adulthood. The first three-fourths of the poem joins together the worlds of the Vietnam War and the segregated Deep South. But it is the burst of closing metaphor in the last eight lines, the passage that begins, "There's more than a nation inside us" that escalates the poem to a level of powerfully compressed insight, which condenses, complicates, and resolves all the themes of the poem. The racially separated soldiers touch and taste each other through the bodies of the bar girls they share, and this erotic communion is further complicated by the image of tunnels, underworlds, and death. In the realms of eros and death, the soldiers are inexorably, unconsciously connected to one another, as they are to their enemies, the Viet Cong soldiers who fought that war in tunnels. The poem that precedes these closing images is effective enough, but it becomes extraordinary when metaphor leaps forward and integrates all levels of the poem with blistering psychic dexterity. This is the image chakra working at full force.

Diction

The ability of images to carry complex information is tremendous. But when the image-making process grows more self-conscious, a poet's attention may shift to the resources of diction. If the instinct underlying image is visual, the instinct underlying diction is not just auditory, as the word implies, but also that of the discriminating intellect, intent upon inflections of weight and implication. Consider "Driving West," by Galway Kinnell:

Sheffield Ghazal 4: Driving West

A tractor-trailer carrying two dozen crushed automobiles
    overtakes a tractor-trailer carrying a dozen new.
Oil is a form of waiting.
The internal combustion engine converts the stasis of
    millennia into motion.
Cars howl on rain-wetted roads.
Airplanes rise through the downpour and throw us through
    the blue sky.
The idea of the airplane subverts earthly life.
Computers can deliver nuclear explosions to precisely
    anywhere on earth.
A lightning bolt is made entirely of error.
Erratic Mercurys and errant Cavaliers roam the highways.
A girl puts her head on a boy's shoulder; they are driving west.
The windshield wipers wipe, homesickness one way, wander-
    lust the other, back and forth.
This happened to your father and to you, Galway—sick to
    stay, longing to come up against the ends of the earth,
    and climb over.

This poem, as it announces more or less explicitly, is about wanderlust, the endless American traveling. And its form of sequential,
at times loosely knit statements (Kinnell's adaptation of the ghazal)
creates intriguing formal effects—those of list and collage. The poem
also usefully displays the meeting ground between image and diction. Here are some lines that initially seem to contain images:

A lightning bolt is made entirely of error.
Erratic Mercurys and errant Cavaliers roam the highways.
A girl puts her head on a boy's shoulder; they are driving west.
The windshield wipers wipe, homesickness one way, wander-
    lust the other, back and forth.

Kinnell "does" image differently from Olds. To begin with the obvious generality, these lines are much more conscious of themselves
as language than Olds's lines. One senses that self-consciousness in a

greater crispness of speech. To say that Kinnell's linguistic resources are *deeper* than those of Olds, though true, doesn't quite get to the heart of the matter. Linguistically, Kinnell's poem distributes the weight of its meaning more widely than Olds's "My Son the Man." In Olds's poem, images carry the emotional and intellectual weight. In Kinnell's poem, aphorism, discourse, and diction share the work with image. His temperament is different from hers; the two poets inhabit different modes.

A good definition of poetic diction is "speech that is consciously making reference to the history of its usage." When a poet of diction employs language, he or she is making reference to the history of its contexts. When Kinnell says, for example, "erratic Mercurys and errant Cavaliers," his wordplay, diction, and punning send roots deep below the alliterative surface, into the earth of the English language with its networks of content and association. These roots require the reader to retrieve and utilize linguistic and mythological memory, and to perform complex cognitions, correlating image, diction, allegory, and analogy all at once. In one fell swoop, Kinnell asks us to summon up and integrate the commercial names of American cars, our knowledge of Roman mythology, and the complex associations of "cavalier" with feudal knighthood, Grail-seeking, chivalry, etc. Likewise, we are ensnared in the recognition that the words *errant, error,* and *erratic* (all used in the space of two lines) spring from the same root, but carry different connotations. *Erratic* means irregular or inconsistent, while *errant* signifies aimlessness or adventurous wandering, and *error* means mistake. In "Driving West," the juxtaposition of these variants creates a rich, arguably precise confusion. Such fine gradients of emphasis are the province of diction.

But Kinnell uses image, too. The line most reminiscent of image in the style of Olds—the simplest, and notably, the most accessible and emotionally evocative moment in the poem, is that of the windshield wipers, sweeping back and forth: "homesickness one way, wanderlust the other." Yet even this metaphor feels *sophisticated* in a way rather different from Olds; it has a flavor of *willful* genius; of mental, not visceral, inventiveness.

The alliterative, aphoristic line, "A lightning bolt is made entirely of error," flirts with image, but swerves toward diction, drawing upon a host of complex references and suggestions. We recall, for example, the folk wisdom that lightning never strikes twice in the same place, and Kinnell asks us to reconstitute that notion (safety, danger) in the context of the poem's theme of wanderlust.

One observable difference between the respective altitudes of image and diction here is that diction (as Kinnell uses it) is intrinsically semantic—a word like *errant* or *wanderlust* calls attention to the writerly act of *choosing.* In that writtenness, the writer is more self-conscious and less impulsive; more editorial and less sheerly imaginative. Kinnell is one of the most passionate of American male poets, but in his diction he is plying fine points of discrimination; employing the words, blade-like, to separate this from that. "Driving West" is a beautiful poem, full of feeling. But writtenness has construed that beauty; it bears the chisel-marks of calculation and self-consciousness, especially in its use of diction.

Diction also, in its exhibition of a speaker making choices, creates the opportunity for the personality of a speaker to figure large in a poem. Such performance of self is visible in the verbal energy of the opening of Dean Young's "Even Funnier Looking Now":

If someone had asked me then,
Do you suffer from the umbrage of dawn's
dark race horses, is your heart a prisoner
of raindrops? Hell yes! I would have said
or No way! Never would I have said,
What could you possibly be talking about?
I had just gotten to the twentieth century
like a leftover girder from the Eiffel Tower.
My Indian name was Pressure–Per-Square-Inch.

Here it is the quirky self of the speaker, manifested in rapid diction shifts, that holds center stage. Intellectual agendas exist in the poem—for example, the speaker's mocking challenge to the aesthetics of poetic elevation—but at a more secondary level than the stage presence of the entertaining and resourceful speaker. It is the cultural and contextual distances between "umbrage" and "Hell yes!," between "dawn" and "Pressure-Per-Square-Inch" that defines this character as both manic and self-conscious. In that sense at least, we might say that the technology of diction enables a writer to manifest more personality than image alone. This suggests, perhaps, that personality only emerges in the higher chakras. Maybe image is, to some degree, a more primal power: thus, more *pre-personality*. From that conclusion we might say that if a young writer considered herself a poet of personality, diction would be one of her preferred tools.

Once again, let us emphasize what should be obvious: although this taxonomy maps a line of increasing poetic sophistication, it is not a hierarchy of ascending poetic quality, or worth. Nor are these tools used in isolation; in good poems, they constantly alternate, intertwine, and fuse.

Rhetoric

What comes next, after image and diction, in this anatomy of poetic powers, might be rhetoric, and it is the thorniest chakra to define. It also seems to be the poetic power that contemporary poets have felt most inhibited about.

Our notions of what the word rhetoric means are various and indistinct. Since rhetoric is described as the art of persuasion, its broadest meaning encompasses all speech acts that take place outside the shower. Most speech is to some degree intended to be persuasive; therefore, most speech has a rhetorical aspect. Every time we use an *although* or *but* in a sentence, we are limiting an assertion to make it more credible to our audience. Every time we provide an example, we are making a case for an argument. Whether you are asking someone to shut the door, or making a remark about weather, you are being rhetorical. Technically, rhetoric contains all the other chakras.

In this context, however, I would like to identify rhetoric with the presence of *gestural* speech: those moments or motions in a poem that have more to do with signifying attitude than delivering information. Such moments are a visible exertion of the speaker's authority, and they ride herd on a poem, directing it while standing aside from it. For example, Larry Levis's poem "A Letter" begins like this:

It's better to have a light jacket on days like this,
Than a good memory.

From such a beginning, anything could follow. Rhetorical gestures create a space in which a poem can take place; they also turn and contour a poem in a way that gives it topography. Rhetoric imparts to a poem what muscle builders call *definition*. A rhetorical moment is a moment of flourish. Of course, such moments have a lot to do with the creation of voice, and of course, diction, image, and statement are also often essential elements of a rhetorical flourish. Nonetheless, I tend to think of rhetoric in terms of *elevation* and gesture. In the Kinnell poem, "Driving West," the moment most easily identified as rhetorical is the closing statement that encompasses and orients the entire preceding procession of stances, contextualizing them in terms of an errant, wandering perceiver.

This happened to your father and to you, Galway

Another familiar example is the end of Robert Hayden's beautiful and well-known poem, "Those Winter Sundays." After the speaker has detailed, in a plain narrative style, the father's domestic chores and the son's ingratitude, he makes a sweeping lyric gesture of rhetorical formality:

What did I know, what did I know
of love's austere and lonely offices?

Hayden's rhetorical question lyrically looks back at its own narrative, at once lamenting and dignifying it. The rhetorical elevation (accompanied by a rise in diction) signifies, of course, the transforming perspective of time: "Then, I knew nothing, but now I know," he says. In that elevation of speech, we recognize the incarnation of the father's loneliness in the speaker and the epiphanic moment of communion. It is also worth noting that though Hayden's gesture is powerful, and though his poem is intensely emotional, in the high formality of the gesture there is also a striking degree of detachment. Rhetoric is impersonal.

Perhaps it is the combination of detachment and forcefulness that explains some of the contemporary reservation about rhetoric. Recent eras in American poetry have been rhetoric-wary. We largely stay away from the grand, the public voice, as if we wanted nothing to do with the dangerous intemperance of speech-making. Ezra Pound, in his Vorticism manifesto, reflects the general prejudicial drift when he says, "The "image" is the furthest possible remove from rhetoric. Rhetoric is the art of dressing up some unimportant matter so as to fool the audience for the time being." Pound's dismissal characterizes rhetoric as inflated and manipulative. Yet there's a hypocrisy, or at least a naïveté in pretending that power is something for poetry to avoid. In fact, power is a source of pleasure, as innately human as sex or food. And as readers, too, don't we know the pleasure of being subject to the power of another?

To repeat: the most visible rhetorical moments are gestural and muscular, shaping space in the poem, and this notion accords with the popular, pejorative descriptive phrases "empty rhetoric" and "merely rhetorical." Such descriptions imply an interior that is vacant. And yes, in fact, the *content* of a rhetorical phrase is often less important than how it *feels* to say or read; rhetoric is the *gesture* itself, and the placement of that gesture in the poem. Rhetoric doesn't add information, it *spin-doctors* what follows or precedes it.

Maybe our popular notions of what rhetoric is are not so wrong.

-It is authoritative and in that sense, willful.
-It is both public and relational in nature.
-It is empty.
-It is muscular and open and defines spaces into which what
  follows flows.

Rhetoric is relational, but it is also public, and formal; it is the affiliate of the pronoun "we," and it provokes the same objections from critics that that plural pronoun does. It is high-handed, didactic, directive, presumptuous, authoritarian.

The two dangers of rhetoric are emptiness and impersonality—the latter because rhetoric is implicitly public in its nature. This might explain, in our period of the American "intimate," "personal" poem, the dearth of rhetorical ingenuity. Both the power and the emptiness of rhetoric can be seen in Wallace Stevens's poem, "The Well Dressed Man with a Beard":

> After the final no there comes a yes
> And on that yes the future world depends.
> No was the night. Yes is this present sun.
> If the rejected things, the things denied,
> Slid over the western cataract, yet one,
> One only, one thing that was firm, even
> No greater than a cricket's horn, no more
> Than a thought to be rehearsed all day, a speech
> Of the self that must sustain itself on speech,
> One thing remaining, infallible, would be
> Enough. Ah! douce campagna of that thing!
> Ah! douce campagna, honey in the heart,
> Green in the body, out of a petty phrase,
> Out of a thing believed, a thing affirmed:
> The form on the pillow humming while one sleeps,
> The aureole above the humming house . . .
>
> It can never be satisfied, the mind, never.

The opening of Stevens's poem is unforgettable in its authority, its cadence, and its inventiveness. It establishes "a space into which what follows flows," and it catches and commands our attention about as well as a poem can. But both the opening and the poem that follows can be used to illustrate the emptiness of rhetoric. Consider what happens if we simply transpose (as memory does sometimes) the terms of this overture: "After the final *yes* there comes a *no,* and on that *no* . . ." Where you might go from there is anybody's guess, but the rhetorical strength is intact because its source is syntactical.

What follows is more problematic. I will always remember the opening and the last line of "Well Dressed Man with a Beard," but the middle of the poem is oddly cluttered and forgettable. It contains Stevens's characteristic weaknesses, a sonorous kind of drumbeating. We are impressed and moved by the overture, but if we track our own listening and comprehending process, the footprints of the poet, as assured as he is, disappear into the bushes, which are also disintegrating.

Though Stevens's poem has rhetorical structure, and plenty of rhythmic cadence, his imagery seems vague and unstructured. This allegedly is a list of things that affirm, that confirm, but they are not themselves *firm*. In all the sound and motion, only the cricket's horn offers us a toehold on that resurrected world. This indeed may be "speech / Of the self that must sustain itself on speech," but it is a frothy, immaterial diet.

Stevens's writing in the middle of the poem reflects, perhaps, the anxious solution of the poet who is rhetorically strong. Like a musician who doesn't have the sheet music in front of him, he just plays *louder;* he salts his monologue with superlatives, like "infallible" and exclamation points; he uses foreign words, he waxes rhapsodic—but the rejected things, the things denied, the *things* upon which so much depends—which are referred to often, and which seem essential to understanding the poem—are never named. The mid-poem is finally private and cerebrally, solipsistically so.

In contrast to Stevens's poem, consider "Trust Me" by Mary Ruefle, a contemporary poet of great rhetorical canniness. Her poem bears some structural similarities to "The Well Dressed Man with a Beard." Ruefle's rhetorical assuredness is evident from the title onward:

Trust Me

What can be discussed in words
I beg to state in brief.
A man has only one death:
it may be as light as goose down
or as heavy as a fatted hog.
Gingerly, the flowers open
and are crushed in the vat.
What's in your new perfume?
The hills of Africa are in it,
and the cormorants with their mouths full of fish,
a bed of carnations, a swannery in Switzerland,
the citrine sun baking Nappa

and a rhino whining at the moon.
An after-dinner argument is in it
and the ever-stronger doses of clap-trap
we are forced to take while still alive.
A whole aeroplane, wings and all,
and the lush spaghetti siphoned into lips
poised for a kiss.
Finish it, finish it.

Like "The Well-Dressed Man with a Beard," the Ruefle poem begins with a charming and commanding manner. Her title and her imperative first sentence may be less oratorically grand than Stevens's, but they are still enormously authoritative. Though the speaker "begs" to state, this begging is *merely* rhetorical—she has the lectern, she has already commanded our attention. Likewise, though she pointedly acknowledges the limitations of speech, she simultaneously asserts her ability not only to encompass those limits, but to do so "in brief." Such confidence is charming as well as powerful. It is an irresistible beginning.

What else the Ruefle poem has in common with Stevens's is the simultaneously large and simple nature of the subject matter: a man's "one death." Following this downbeat piece of information is a list—again, structurally, this is close to the Stevens poem—a list of things to live for, a list of implicit affirmations, of things balanced in the scales against the fact of death—things that, in their vividness, variety, and number especially, outweigh the *one* death.

In marked contrast to "The Well Dressed Man with a Beard," Ruefle's list is both concrete and exotic. Moreover, with a lexicon of skilled touches, she makes her connection to the reader personal, more so than Stevens. This movement toward the reader is important after her imperious and didactic opening. One way she warms the poem up a bit is by manipulating the pronouns: the speaker-centered (I) poem turns toward the *you*, then into the collective *we*. In this sense, Ruefle has it all over Stevens; for though, like Stevens, she is temperamentally a solipsist, an improviser, and a monologuist, she has a strong sense of rhetoric as *connective*.

Ruefle's poem also has a clear, if associative, internal logic, embodied in the discursive interplay between rhetoric and image. After the blunt announcement of her subject, Death, she embodies her theme with the image of flowers being crushed. From here on, the dominant trope of the poem becomes the manufacture of perfume, whose ingredients contain, apparently, everything on earth, plain and fancy. *What do you do with perfume?* the allegory implicitly asks, and the answer is, *Enjoy it.* Though by the poem's conclusion, the activity of soul-making has metamorphosed into eating a spaghetti dinner, we understand the command: to clean our plates.

Both Stevens and Ruefle use rhetorical muscle to reach for ecstasy in their poems, but Ruefle's wildness, represented by her rich, sudden catalogue, is framed and supported by an interlocking complex of logic, image, and tone that carries the reader over the associative jumps.

Rhetoric is intrinsically public: civil, civic, and civilizing. One evidence of that can be found in the rituals of public life that structure private life. The wedding ceremony, for example, is rhetorical: do you take this person to have and to hold, in sickness and health, for richer for poorer, for better and for worse—a classic use of antithesis to encompass possibility. By contrast, a divorce is a mere procedure, not a ceremony; though it is legally formal, it signifies a dissolution of structure, and therefore does not require the sanctions of ritual music or the gestures and flourishes of rhetoric.

One group of American poets that has not abandoned rhetoric is the postmodern cadre, and they make an interesting sidebar to this discussion. In John Ashbery's well-known poem "Decoy," the first twelve lines of which are below, we find the rhetorical spirit gone mad:

> We hold these truths to be self-evident:
> That ostracism, both political and moral, has
> Its place in the twentieth-century scheme of things;
> That urban chaos is the problem we have been seeing into and
>   seeing into,
> For the factory, deadpanned by its very existence into a
> Descending code of values, has moved right across the road
>   from total financial upheaval

And caught regression head-on. The descending scale does
    not imply
A corresponding deterioration of moral values, punctuated
By acts of corporate vandalism every five years,
Like a bunch of violets pinned to a dress, that knows and
    ignores its own standing.
There is every reason to rejoice with those self-styled prophets
    of commercial disaster, those harbingers of gloom,
Over the imminent lateness of the denouement that, advanc-
    ing slowly, never arrives,

Ashbery is celebrated for his rhetorical virtuosity and, because of its declarative authority and its cannibalized bureaucratic diction, Ashbery's poem *feels* like it makes sense. Because it borrows familiar public language and cadences (the American Declaration of Independence), it sounds like a public lecture; but it is all, as the honest title implies, a decoy. In the wending and winding of rhetoric and reference, Ashbery implies that such structures of speech are empty, a decorative pretext for our living. His rhetorical acrobatics are stage props, his apparent logic is a ceremony of deconstructed disaffection. For all its gesturing, "Decoy" is representative of our total disenchantment with the *ends* of rhetoric: Ashbery is not trying to instruct, persuade, or emote. It is poetry in the way that elevator music is music, whipped cream poured onto a cake that is not there.

Ashbery may not believe in Truth, nor, exactly, in emotional persuasion, nor even in identity, except as an interesting and shifting fiction that happens to run our lives. But he definitely believes in rhetoric and its infinitely entertaining variety. He is often a poet of wit, though he is too muscular a poet to be consigned to that category effectively. In "Decoy," he maintains his own brand of textural firmness (which the Stevens poem does not) throughout.

An important commonality between the poems by Ashbery and Ruefle is their great playfulness with identity. That playfulness can be connected to their rhetoricity as poets—the one is source and result of the other. And here is one explanation for the lack of rhetorical experiment in much contemporary work: we are constrained by our belief in the precious individuality of the poet, and by our conviction that poetry equals sincerity. We are oddly ready to become poets by getting down and dirty with the details of our private lives, but oddly unwilling to get lofty and public in our speech.

If the image chakra is pre-personality, we could say that the rhetoric chakra is post-personality. Our resistance to employing the impersonal nature of rhetoric (or our reactive distaste for it) accounts for the contemporary scarcity of poetic rhetoricians. The protectiveness and sanctity with which we regard our contemporary notion of the Self, plus our understandable cautiousness about the wielding of Power combine to make much contemporary poetry rhetoric-poor. The objective of rhetoric is, almost comically, the opposite of the goal of therapy: not to understand oneself, but to manipulate others.

To think of other rhetorically strong poets—Marianne Moore, Stevens, Yeats, Auden—is to realize that we actually have very little idea of *who* they were as people. One has a sense of their character, and their authority, as manifested in their poems, one has a sense of their exhalations, but they themselves are concealed or protected from our scrutiny, in a way that, say, Philip Levine or Sharon Olds are not.

Rhetoric has been a skill in atrophy in contemporary poetry. Maybe our American cult of individuality, our obsession with identity as a sort of divinely granted personal possession, makes us suspicious of the study of writerly techniques. Yet rhetorical facility is a sort of index of relative power—the shy, the earnest, the low-to-the-ground can be distinguished from the lofty, the free, the assertive by their relation to rhetorical authority. There is a quality of boldness and freedom in some poems and poets that others seem never to attain. The instinct for rhetoric is often a defining factor.

Bringing It All Back Home

A taxonomic essay like this one suggests that poetic techniques are compartmentalized, like a tool box from which the poet draws one tool at a time—hammer, socket wrench, chisel. But a poem like Paul Goodman's "Birthday Cake" displays how various and expressive a poem can be. Here all the altitudes are in play; as a result the poem has not just great visceral force and urgency, but intellectual precision and a rhetorical persuasiveness. Goodman's poem shows how a strong sensibility can fashion something forceful, discriminating, and intuitive, out of the given poetic tools of rhetoric, diction, and image:

Birthday Cake

> Now isn't it time
> when the candles on the icing
> are one two too many
> too many to blow out
> too many to count too many
> isn't it time to give up this ritual?
>
> although the fiery crown
> fluttering on the chocolate
> and through the darkened room advancing
> is still the most loveliest sight
> among our savage folk
> that have few festivals.
>
> But the thicket is too hot and thick
> and isn't it time, isn't it time
> when the fires are too many
> to eat the fire and not the cake
> and drip the fires from my teeth
> as once I had my hot hot youth.

Goodman's poem seems, at first, dominantly rhetorical. The first stanza opens with the formal, authoritative question, a speech-gesture that willfully implies its own answer ("Yes, it is time to give up this ritual"). Thus we might initially suspect the poem of being overcontrolled, too willful. Yet we quickly sense, from the plaintive, repetitive simplicity of its vocabulary and the broke-down, run-on syntax, that the poem is driven by the speaker's feverish emotion. The rushing plaintive phrases are the unpunctuated speech of the child self: *I-don't wanna I don't-wanna,* unconcerned with grammatical correctness. The grammar of the id is always simple: subject-verb, subject-verb—and the dominant energy of stanza one is *id-ish*.

The second stanza of Goodman's poem, enclosed in that familiar appliance of the essay, a qualifying clause, is of a distinctly different altitude. If the first stanza is urgent with feeling and minimal in information, the second stanza is packed with information, carried by both imagery and diction. Grammatically elaborate, sophisticated in temper and technique, it is a lyrical essay in six lines.

What is that information? That the rituals of culture (including birthday cakes) are ancient and indispensable. In part, this message is carried by imagery. The imagery—"fire," "crown," "dark room"—carries not just a perceptual intensity but a rich evocation of cultural history—the feudal resonances of crowns and fire are communal and sacred. And the dark room itself suggests a cavernous, pre-electric setting, where savage folk (and children) gather for collective warmth and ceremony.

Diction also directs our attention toward shared memory. We are reminded of the roots of ritual, not just by "crown" but by "festival" and "folk." It is we contemporary folk, the narrator says, stripped of ritual life, who are savage. Diction shifts upward in stanza two. So does syntax. The syntax of stanza two is processional and elaborate, as it needs to be to carry so much information. Most especially wonderful is the iambic, formal inversion of line three: not "moving through the dark room," but "and through the darkened room advancing." It is a coronation procession; also, perhaps, a kind of military assault, with its strong cadence and the suggestive choice of "advance."

In this stanza the speaker rises above the petty self-concern of the aging, childishly resentful speaker and considers the welfare of the culture as a whole, which he sympathetically recognizes is "savage" and therefore in need of preservation and sponsorship. Is it coincidence that the "small" self is transcended in the most formalized speech of the poem?

Just a vestige, a shred of the child-self remains visible in stanza two, in that lovely double-superlative adjective, "most loveliest sight"—a moment of affectionate gush that communicates the simple, unsophisticated love of fire and chocolate in a dark room.

The third and final stanza of "Birthday Cake" descends again to the level of the plaintive, imperative id, into the "thicket" of intense emotion, back to the repetitious, the pell-mell anxious voice. Again, the speech becomes largely monosyllabic. But in stanza three, anxiety is transformed from self-pity to anger, and the speaker's helplessness is brilliantly transmuted into a formulation of action—to eat the fire and not the cake.

In this final imaginative act of enormous sophistication and completeness, the poem resoundingly answers the question it began with—Is it time to give up this ritual? No, says the poem—rather, it is time to *revise* the ritual in a glorious, self-destructive and vitality-affirming spectacle. Here, the aging king of the ego eats his crown, affirms his virility and concedes his absurdity all at once. This promised act is at once comic, exhibitionistic, and triumphant. This too is a ceremony, and its naturalness, breadth, and coherence—like the poem itself—is extraordinary. It is a double triumph of id and super-ego at once, and a home run for the culture.

What Goodman's poem demonstrates is how skills are combined and integrated by a strong poet into powerful, unprecedented poetry. "Birthday Cake" is not in the least cerebral, but it is hugely intelligent. It is full of feeling and fully engaged in that feeling, but it also offers shifting perspective on its feeling. In the fluctuating alloy of image, diction, and rhetoric, it persuades us of its sincerity and its comprehension.

In some ways this essay means to exhort us toward the use of more sophisticated, authoritarian, and artificial poetic means. But Goodman's poem, with its mixture of savagery and sophistication, is also a powerful reminder of another indispensable poetic element: quantity of force. If eloquence means lofty and denatured, eloquence is not the goal. Technique is nothing without passion to animate it. Still, to entertain the possibilities for technical authority—to have access to all the chakras and all the altitudes—is to be able to imagine the possibility of continued growth for ourselves as writers. That dream of growth is essential for any artist. To preserve that dream through thick and thin is a kind of talent, too, one that might enable us to move past the artist we thought we were, into some new identity—perhaps less familiar but more wonderful.

"'Tis Backed Like a Weasel"

THE SLIPPERINESS OF METAPHOR

1. Cloud

There is something irreconcilably, neurologically primal about the act of metaphor. This primal wildness conceals it from us. Of the hinterlands of the gray matter, where metaphors roam free, our data is all rumor, conjecture, and anecdote. Because metaphorical speech is such a commonplace, because almost anyone can and does produce metaphor on a daily basis, we assume that it is scrutable. Because it is a mental process, because it takes place inside our own heads (on our property), because it leaves our own authorial lips, we assume we know something of its workings. But we do not. Invariably, the only adequate way to describe the metaphorical event is by another metaphor. It is a mystery hand going into a black mystery box. The head says, "Fetch me a metaphor, hand," and the hand disappears under a cloth. A moment later, the hand reappears, metaphor on its extended palm. But, despite the spontaneity and ease of this event, we have only a vague idea of where the image came from. In fact, we don't know. And neither does the hand.

What we do know about metaphor is that it is the raw uranium of poetry, and that an urge to claim wild similarities is one of the earliest markers of the poetic spirit. It is a striking fact that some people, otherwise very intelligent and artistic, seem devoid of metaphorical ability, as if that gene were simply missing from their chromosomes. In this way metaphor seems truly a *gift;* that is, something given, not earned. Aristotle said that he could teach you to write a play, he could teach you beginning / middle / end, he could teach you the parts of rhetoric, but he could not teach anyone to make a metaphor. Hemingway didn't have it or didn't want it—and became the archangel of American realism. In poetry, William Carlos Williams— our red wheelbarrow—is the figure we have nominated as our token realist, and though this reputation is not entirely deserved, it is true that Williams is a man of images, but not metaphor. Emerson had it, and metaphor flows out of him like Perrier from some high Swiss alp. Emerson's essays, which are his real poetry, seem basically the result of holding a bottle under that transcendental faucet: all the essays say the same two things (know your worth / try harder), but they say it with enormous figurative variety. Emerson is an amazing and persuasive metaphorical thinker, not a logical one; to read him is to enter into a state of drunkenness, which suggests something about the disorienting nature of metaphor. The beginning of his essay "Experience" goes like this:

> We wake and find ourselves on a stair; there are stairs below
> us, which we seem to have ascended, and there are stairs
> above us, many a one, which go upward and out of sight. . . .
> Sleep lingers all our lifetime about our eyes, as night hovers
> all day in the boughs of the fir-tree. All things swim and glit-
> ter. Our life is not so much threatened as our perception.

Over the years, I have read "Experience" a half dozen times, and yet I must confess that I cannot recall what Emerson's main point about Experience is. Still, the image of those stairs lingers in my mind, an analogue for strange wakefulness in midlife. This fact, that metaphors can be separated from their contexts, that they often seem to function independently of the rest of the work they belong to, suggests that metaphors often have an irregular, almost autonomous relationship to their texts, whether that text is a poem, a story or, in this case, an essay.

Stephen Dobyns, in his excellent essay, "Metaphor and the Authenticating Act of Memory," provides a sturdy definition of the well-governed metaphor. A functional metaphor, from this perspective, is a little engine of equivalence:

> Generally . . . [metaphors] are forms of comparison that
> exist to heighten the object of the comparison. . . . A meta-
> phor consists of the object half and the image half. . . . Since
> the object half of the metaphor attempts to provide a context
> for the image, the object itself should be easily discoverable.

All right: the "equation" of a functional metaphor consists of an object half and an image half. In Robert Lowell's metaphor, "a Sahara of snow," for example, *snow*, the object, provides the context for Sahara, the image. If a metaphor works well, the two images appear simultaneously in the mind, suspended in a field of parallel resonance. There is an equivalence between them, but also a hierarchy. In Lowell's metaphor, *snow* possesses a primary status, as the object half. Our quick trip to the Sahara lends us a perspective upon the snow, connotating vastness and barrenness.

Czselaw Milosz's poem, "The Fall," which states its premise in the first line, provides a lucid extended example of metaphor in action:

> The death of a man is like the fall of a mighty nation
> That had valiant armies, captains, and prophets,
> And wealthy ports and ships over all the seas,
> But now it will not relieve any besieged city,
> It will not enter into any alliance,
> Because its cities are empty, its population dispersed,
> Its land once bringing harvest is overgrown with thistles,
> Its mission forgotten, its language lost,
> The dialect of a village high upon inaccessible mountains.

Here we see precisely the perspective-granting function of metaphor, as described in Dobyns's definition. As the metaphor of "The

Fall" extends and unfolds, our understanding of what a man's death means deepens and expands, through one analogical particularity after another. Moreover, as we refer back and forth between the object and the images, we are guided to reflect upon what life consists of: friendship ("alliances"), the potential for doing good ("relief of besieged cities"), etc.

And the closing image in Milosz's final line is psychologically eloquent of both the finality and the mysteriousness of that loss; the dead one is now remote and forever inaccessible to the living. The image of a village lost in unreachable mountains performs its work with a coherence that seems natural and effortless, yet complex with implications. At the close of the poem we hold two images simultaneously in our mind's eye: dead man and abandoned, barren country.

A metaphor goes out and comes back; it is a fetching motion of the imagination. Jack of Jack and the Beanstalk fame was a metaphor-maker in that sense: sent forth with the family cow, he was supposed to translate it into money. But Jack strayed sideways: he looked at some beans and saw wild visions of something else. His is a tale of irresponsibility rewarded. Here is Rilke's own slightly disordered image of fetching, from the *Ninth Duino Elegy:*

For the wanderer doesn't bring from the mountain slope
a handful of earth to the valley, untellable earth, but only
some word he has won, a pure word, the yellow and blue
gentian.

Rilke's analogy is powerful, but also illogical—he is speaking of what can be retained of any experience: only a *word*, which is also a *flower*, which stands for the *handfuls of earth* we can't bring back . . . huh? The same metaphor one understands clearly enough while reading the poem may slide around under inspection.

Effective metaphors are always more complicated than we suppose. Their bright, singular quality, that endorphin-like impact, which strikes so swiftly and so hard, like a happy blow on the head, makes us believe that they are simple. Also, their nature as *equations* misleads us to suppose that they are the servants of logic. Snow=Sahara. Dead man=fallen nation. But a fine metaphor exceeds logic in odd ways.

2. Whale

The problem—and the glory—of metaphor is that it is an intuitive brain function being temporarily employed by a rational one. In its function of equivalence, the metaphor is held *responsible* to logic and correlation. Metaphor is produced by one part of the brain and interrogated by another. It is a lateral function that theoretically must fit into a forward movement. It is a vertical spike on a horizontal time line. It is a digression that must be squeezed neatly into an argument.

But the edges never get fully tucked in. There are always loose threads, as in Billy Collins's excellent poem "Man in Space":

All you have to do is listen to the way a man
sometimes talks to his wife at a table of people
and notice how intent he is on making his point
even though her lower lip is beginning to quiver,

and you will know why the women in science
fiction movies who inhabit a planet of their own
are not pictured making a salad or reading a magazine
when the men from earth arrive in their rocket,

why they are always standing in a semicircle
with their arms folded, their bare legs set apart,
their breasts protected by hard metal disks.

The analogy in "Man in Space" is highly functional: the image half, the description of the defensive Amazon space women, interacts creatively with the object half of the drama in a way that resonantly exposes the situation for the reader. The equivalence is not just clear and rational, but surprising and joyful in its strangeness. There is what our critic-shaman Robert Bly would call a *leap* in this poem. Here the object half is "how women feel"; the image is, of course, the Amazon space women. We go out and refer back; in fact, we go back and forth—from situation to image to situation—and the movement is very satisfying. The work the metaphor does, the poet doesn't need to: he doesn't need to state his thesis: "Women have so much legitimate reason to resent men, or wives their husbands, that if they had their own planet, they would not allow men onto it." What happens in the image is more vivid, playful, and complex than any discursive formulation. The image does the work.

And yet, and yet—when a ship goes to another country and then returns, it always brings some kind of foreign vegetation attached to its hull. Under the waterline, some zebra mussel or termite is hunkered in the dark—and a metaphor, too, will always return from its journey with something unintended attached. In the Collins poem, which seems so tidy, so well "closed," we have the odd sexual subtext of the images—the spread legs and the shiny breasts of the Amazon women. These details probably come from the 1950s science-fiction movies that are the cultural source of Collins's image. Those movies were made, after all, by men, not women, and the result is the oddly confusing image of proto-feminist go-go dancers. It's Barbarella night at the Playboy Mansion! Although this is a poem of feminist empathy, it totes some funny baggage with it. (And doesn't it also, by the way, suggest that women are aliens?) In this sense, metaphors, like prescription drugs, should probably carry a warning label about possible side effects. A label on the Collins poem might say, "Warning: this politically correct poem could prolong your sexism."

This is always going to be the case; unintended adjunct qualities will always attach themselves to metaphors. A metaphor's luminosity lies not just in its equivalency but also in its unmanageability.

Popular culture abounds with other examples. When Mae West makes her famous remark, "Is that a gun in your pocket or are you just glad to see me?" the subtext is pretty spooky, suggesting as it does that male genitals are a deadly weapon. Another troubling public use of metaphor is the well-meaning bumper sticker often seen on the cars of educators, the one that says, "A mind is like a parachute: it only works if it's open." Sounds good, for a second. But what about the peripheral implication of this analogy: that the body is plummeting toward the ground at tremendous speed? And if it is, after all, are we supposed to think the mind is really going to save it?

The point is that more irregularity resides in the process of metaphor than we credit with our definitions and our ideas of proper function. If metaphor provides another level to a poem, and it does, it is not always exactly *supplemental*. The added level itself has levels within it. The mind moves back and forth between the object and the image and forth and back and what is inside and outside, foreground or background, often becomes unclear.

Here's a poem that illustrates the fantastic elasticity of metaphor, and some of its disorienting properties. The poem is "A Long Commute" by Laura Kasischke, one of the premier image-makers of my generation:

Faith is a long commute. Lots
of time to change
the station on the radio, time
to relive the past, to consider

the future the way
the boy in the bus station
standing by the trashcan
the afternoon the bomb went off
must have had time to consider

his own hands carefully in his hands. The road

is narrow and it goes

straight through the gardens of Paradise. Lots

of soggy godhearts dripping
blood on their bloody vines. Behind me

a beautiful blind girl carries a Bible
home in a plastic bag, while

before me, an old
woman and her old mother
drive a Cadillac over
the flowers slowly.

Kasischke establishes her presiding metaphor in the first line, and we interrogate it for equivalence: What does "a commute" mean, we ask, in the context of faith? Well, it is a kind of *going to work*, an equivalence we can entertain. But the sequence of images that follows the opening assertion is dreamy, peculiar, and expansive—images so rich and particular they effectively displace our memory of the poem's alleged theme. In fact, we forget their metaphorical status. These images in their alternate world take on independent lives, which we only intermittently refer to our alleged thesis. We could call this allegory, but that term only partially accommodates the dark surrealism of the poem. What is the "equivalence," for example, of the image of the blind girl carrying a Bible in a plastic bag? What about the soggy godhearts dripping on their vines?

Kasischke's metaphors have a daring recklessness that has to do with her intuitive method; hers is a temperament less governed by precise equivalence than by a surrender to the riptides of psyche. This is the dream-realm beloved by Freud and Magritte. And finally, this hallucinatory narrative-allegory inside the image half of the metaphor is mysterious in a way that the Collins poem isn't because it comes from another temperament—one with a different, more rhapsodic (and surrealist) relationship to metaphor.

For the purposes of this essay, Kasishcke's poem shows that equivalence is a limited concept when it comes to metaphor. If, in some hands, metaphor is employed on a mission of *perspective*, i.e., a moving away from a thing in order to see it better—Kasischke's "A Long Commute" illustrates the equally operative power of *fantasy* in metaphor-making. Such fantasy is not solely about "bringing back" the resources of the imagination to enrich realism, but about bending the real into a different shape.

Kasischke's poem elicits a significant issue, an inevitable issue in regard to metaphor: the competition between a local moment in a poem and the poem as a whole. This tension between the localized textual pleasures of image and the global economy of the poem are addressed in part by Mary Oliver in her statement about imagery from her book on craft, *A Poetry Handbook:*

There are no rules about using imagery. Certainly it enlivens and deepens the poem. It is a source of delight. It makes the

poem more meaningful—more of an experience. It is powerful stuff.

How much one uses it is a matter of taste. The writer
would be wise to remember, however, just how much
emotional excitement it can create. The poem that, all
along its line of endeavor, pauses to give out "jolts" of imagery may end up like a carnival ride: the reader has been
lurched, and has laughed—has been all but whiplashed—
but has gotten nowhere. In the shed electricity of too
much imagery the purpose of the ride—and a sense of
arrival—may be lost.

There is also the question of imagery that is fit and imagery
that may be unfit. This too is a matter of taste. Poetry is a serious business. . . . It is joyful, and funny too sometimes, but it
is neither facile nor poisonous. If you are not sure your imagery is appropriate, don't use it.

Oliver may come off here as the Miss Manners of poetic convention, but she represents one traditional position regarding image,
and, by proxy, metaphor: too much local "excitement" can under-
mine the poem's architecture as a whole and in some way damage
its cumulative power. The social analogy might be that if an individual metaphor has too much personality, it can imbalance the social
structure of the entire poem.

Interestingly, when metaphor is subordinated to the designs of the
poem as a whole, as Oliver advocates, it often shifts grammatically
from the position of being a freestanding noun or phrase to the verb
or adjective position. In such forms it becomes less vertical and more
horizontal, relative to the forward movement of the poem. Here, in the
beginning of the Robert Hass poem "Interrupted Meditation," we can
see the speaker thinking hard about the proper status of metaphor:

Little green involute fronds of fern at creekside.
And the sinewy clear water rushing over creekstone
of the palest amber, veined with a darker gold,
thinnest lines of gold rivering through the amber
like—ah, now we come to it. *We were not put on earth,*
the old man said,

. . . .

to express ourselves.

The water is *sinewy,* and the creekstone is *veined* and *rivered*—
there are metaphors aplenty here. And yet the speaker seems to consider these grammatically buried metaphors as qualitatively different
from the more overt simile he is tempted to make, then turns back
from making, with the open-ended, interrupted "like."

It is a significant distinction. The simile, Hass guiltily implies,
would be an act of self-expression and thus of self-glorification. Such
a metaphor would be categorically different from the metaphors already buried in the text of his description. These buried metaphors
are unobtrusive, chosen in a spirit of representational fidelity, and,
though they supplement and augment the poem's discourse in subtle
ways, they do not take a dramatically active role in the poem; they
don't proclaim their singularity. In that way, they seem to be of a different species from, for example, the metaphors in the poems by
Collins and Kasischke.

3. Weasel

In its conservative function of equivalence, metaphor is used as a clarifying, focusing device. If we think of a poem as a social act, we could
say that the poem as a whole is responsible to the reader, and that the
success of the poem is measurable by the reader's ability to "reliably"
inhabit its comparisons. Metaphor may be, in such an enterprise, an
enriching device, but it must not toss the rider from the horse.

In contrast, when metaphor is employed in its more fantastic
function, its validity might be said to lie in its exhibition of impul-
siveness, as in this fragment of Andre Breton's "Postman Cheval":

We are the sighs of the glass statue that raises itself on its
    elbow when man sleeps
And shining holes appear in his bed
Holes through which stags with coral antlers can be seen in
    a glade
And naked women at the bottom of a mine

Breton's subject is the inner world, the self-creating imagination, in motion; to him, the social world, including any anxiety about accommodating the reader's comprehension, is irrelevant. In the Surrealist aesthetic, imagery has virtue to the extent that it exhibits freedom, and art is "reliable" to the extent that it trusts in the revelation of process. The poem is an action, not an object, and its architecture is a series of moment-to-moment jolts and explosions.

But for both the conservative and the radical poet, there is in the use of metaphor something faintly opposed to reality. Somber or joyful, rational or surreal, descriptive or fantastic, a metaphor is intrinsically a breaking away from fidelity and continuity, an allergic reaction to too much reality. Something there is that doesn't love an equal sign. Or, to refer back to the Collins poem, "Man in Space," we could say that in every metaphor there is a tension between the forces of gravity and antigravity, between the marriage to realism and the infidelity of fantasy. What is gravity but a mean husband? What is freedom but the right to repel all boarders?

Something of this tension between the social and the imaginative is visible in one of the most notorious scenes from *Hamlet:* Act 3, Scene 2, a scene in which Polonius has come to summon Hamlet to an audience with his mother. The situation of the play is that everyone is worried about Hamlet's dangerous volatility; he is a wild card, and they are lobbying both to "read" him and to tame him; they want him to get with the collective program, but he keeps rebuffing their approaches:

Polonius: My lord, the queen would speak with you,
   and presently.
Hamlet: Do you see yonder cloud that's almost in shape of
   a camel?
Polonius: By the mass and 'tis like a camel, indeed.
Hamlet: Methinks it is like a weasel.
Polonius: It is backed like a weasel.
Hamlet: Or like a whale?
Polonius: Very like a whale.
Hamlet: Then I will come to my mother by and by. (Aside) They
   fool me to the top of my bent. I will come by and by.

Polonius: I will say so.
Hamlet: By and by is easily said.

It is easy in this scene to see Polonius as a doddering, people-pleasing, ill-used fool, and Hamlet as a mocking, arrogant youth. What is not so obvious is that Polonius himself, in his spineless agreeable way, is insidious, an agent of the status quo. For if he is trying to please by agreeing, he is also trying to draw Hamlet's imagination into consensus, into the social web. If only Polonius can get agreement about those clouds, Hamlet can be potentially harnessed into the collective agenda.

But Hamlet, that subversive figure, that poet, will not cooperate—he continuously changes his images, and by implication shape-shifts himself, moving out of reach. Hamlet's behavior, his insistence on difference, represents the antisocial impulse in metaphor, which speeds away from social reality. Hamlet's weapon against the forces that wish to "make him sane," to get real, is metaphor. Metaphor is both weapon and shield for the person who would protect himself from too much reality or from the wrong kind of reality—it creates a buffer zone of imaginative negotiability. And it protects his right to dream, which, like all freedoms, is dangerous.

Three Tenors

PINSKY, HASS, GLÜCK, AND THE
DEPLOYMENT OF TALENT

The artistic life begins in instinct and moves toward calculation; or maybe, it begins in blind obsession and ends in self-possession. Or does it begin in play and end in ambition? Or, some say, it begins in inspiration and moves toward repetition. Whichever version you subscribe to, the loss of innocence is inevitable, and it is indeed a loss—but one that has its compensations. Some of the names for that compensation are skill, perspective, and choice.

The stories of poetic transformation are the legends of the craft: Yeats's renunciation of romance in his fifties; Adrienne Rich's defiant rejection of the polished patriarchal conventions of her apprenticeship; C. K. Williams's poetical conversion from the 1970s idiom of quasi-surrealism to the complex, discursive sentences of *With Ignorance* and *Tar*. The case histories of repetition are also well known: poets who seem caught, tethered to a subject or style from which they cannot depart.

As a reader, to be delivered a good poet book-by-book is an

enthralling drama. One comes to recognize the athleticism and re-silience required of the serious poet, the physical and spiritual re-sourcefulness, the ways in which fixity of character and self-renewal are sometimes at odds, the way obsession struggles against and then suddenly, sometimes, collaborates with discovery. "Professional poet" is a laughable expression, but perhaps it is in the throes of self-alteration that a poet proves herself or himself most professional.

But the resources required to reconfigure a talent are quite dis-tinct from the ones required to discover a first way of writing. The veteran artist knows so much more than the apprentice, has so much more craft at his / her disposal, better understands the panorama of possibility. But she also knows more about mere competence and about the elusiveness of the radiant thing itself. To revise artistic di-rection requires not the lunging, half-ignorant zeal of the beginner, but a knowledgeable unmaking, a cold self-assessment and slow re-conception. Strategic intelligence is one of those essential, rarely mentioned dimensions of talent, unromantic as a T square, but with-out it, change is a guessing game. Everyone has a nose, said Auden, but not everyone knows where to point it.

Helen Vendler, in her book *The Breaking of Style: Hopkins, Heaney, Graham,* draws an analogy that underscores the drama of such changes:

> When a poet puts off an old style (to speak for a moment as
> though this were a deliberate undertaking), he or she perpe-
> trates an act of violence . . . on the self. It is not too much to
> say that the old body must be dematerialized if the poet is to
> assume a new one. . . . The fears and regrets attending the act
> of permanent stylistic change can be understood by analogy
> with divorce, expatriation, and other such painful spiritual or
> imaginative departures. It is hoped, of course, that the new
> body—like the new spouse or the new country—will be more
> satisfactory than the old, but it is a hope, not a certainty.

The three poets discussed here—Robert Pinsky, Robert Hass, and Louise Glück—are among the most resilient of American writers. Prominent members of their generation, all three have fashioned size-able, rich bodies of work. Their material success—publication, prizes, and status—is the stuff of book jackets, but on a more impressive level, their significance has been registered by readers. Each of these poets has written touchstone poems, whose appearance has rippled through our poetry culture: Hass's "Meditation at Lagunitas," Pinsky's "Shirt," and Glück's "Mock Orange" are some easily named examples.

Each of these three careers also displays an intense, ongoing meditation about form and subject matter. One feels that each poet has confronted the fixedness of a poetic identity and managed to break it open, to begin again. Hass and Pinsky, in very distinct ways, have explored the limits of conversational meditation and gone beyond them. Glück, after succeeding brilliantly at dramatic monologue in its received forms, has extended and deepened its range. Their transformations tell us something about the dogged, wrangling journey of the artist.

Robert Pinsky: Glittering Appetite

Robert Pinsky is a much stranger poet than is generally acknowledged. As the U.S. poet laureate from 1997 to 2000, he has been such a skilled diplomat that people have automatically assumed his poetry to be also civic or democratic. His public articulateness, the communal role he has argued for American poetry, and his personal charisma likewise seem to have cast a spell on the reading public, convincing them that Pinsky the poet is some sort of Horace or Whitman. The truth is more complicated. True, Pinsky eloquently argues for the innately civic function of poetry. But Pinsky the poet has been an innovative, deeply eccentric, and anomalous presence in American poetry. Restlessness has been a large part of his story: his own poetry embodies dramatic shifts of style, from the fluent discursive values of his first several books, to the highly compacted, intensely lyrical, sometimes hermetic, fabrications of his later work.

In the long discursive poem of his second book, *An Explanation of America,* and in his essays in *The Situation of Poetry*, Pinsky is an authoritative exponent of the sense-making, essayistic conversational aspect of poetry. Written in 1976, the title essay in *The Situation of Poetry* is an ars poetica:

"Discursive". . . . the word signifies going through or going over one's subject. Whether digressively or directly, at a walk

or at a run, the motion is on the ground and by foot, putting
its weight part by part onto the terrain to be covered. Such
a method tends to be inclusive; it tends to be the opposite of
intuitive.

It even tends to be earnest . . . it is primarily neither ironic
nor ecstatic. . . . The idea is to have all of the virtues of prose,
in addition to those qualities and degrees of precision which
can be called poetic.

Even in this description of an aesthetic he advocates, Pinsky
seems to be suggesting its limitations, what it is not: not intuitive but
reasoned; not "fancy" but earnest; not emphatically witty but plain.
Neither ironic nor ecstatic. Possibly even, as his metaphor acknowledges, pedestrian.

Yet Pinsky's own discursive early work is swift and protean. In
a passage from the long inventive title poem of "An Explanation of
America," the speaker attempts to name what a culture—in particular, what American culture—is:

A country is the things it wants to see.
If so, some part of me, though I do not,
Must want to see these things—as if to say:

"I want to see the calf with two heads suckle;
I want to see the image of a woman
In rapid sequence of transparencies
Projected on a bright flat surface, conveying
The full illusion and effect of motion,
In vast, varying scale, with varying focus,
Swallow the image of her partner's penis.
I want to see enormous colored pictures
Of people with impossible complexions,
. . . .
I want to see men playing games with balls.

Not without wit (the droll contrast between diction and subject in
the description of pornography), or speed, or surprise, or manifold
catalogues of tactile data, "An Explanation of America" is nonetheless

certainly essayistic, governed by the patient, capacious rationality of a speaker who knows and declares his own intentions. As he says later in the same passage, "I want our country like a common dream / To be between us in what we want to see—" That notion of commonality, of the poet as tribal sense-maker, persists in Pinsky's work, though the method of the poems transforms substantially.

What would, for example, the earlier Pinsky have made of the dense, vatic, incantatory, somewhat hermetic poem "Hut," which, like many of Pinsky's later poems, plunges into a clipped dense set of vocables without much explanatory preparation?

> Nothing only
> what it was—
>
> Slates, burls, rims:
>
> Their names like the circus
> Lettering on a van: *Bros.* and *Movers*
> Symmetrical buds of
> Meaning in the spurs and serifs
> Of scarlet with gold outlines.
>
> Transport and Salvage,
> Moving and Storage.
>
> The house by the truck yard:
> *Flag walk. Shake siding.* The frontyard spruce
> A hilt of shadows.

This brief passage shows the same investigative spirit about the world that motivates and animates Pinsky's early work, but the poet's style of presentation has changed: from a conversational style of casual explication to a more incantatory, impersonal form of enunciation. The discursive lubrication with which the earlier Pinsky presented the poem has been replaced by a love of abruptness, collision, and collage. Grammatically, this transformation is evidenced in the shift from long unwinding sentences to clipped, short units of lyric fragment that don't explain themselves, and that are not even formalized by an article. He has gone, one might say from explicator to gnostic namer, from the secular, discursive Horatian thinker-poet to the more declarative role of tribal priest-poet, one who ushers us toward Mystery. Pinsky's later poems, some of them at least, have assumed the very characteristics he once enumerated as nondiscursive: they are intuitive and ecstatic.

The particular province of Pinsky's vision, his great topic, is the project of Culture: its manifold forms and origins, its encoded heritages and layerings. He is fascinated by the way the physical and the spiritual shape each other in joists and pottery, typographical fonts and dentures. His visionary contribution to that topic is to represent how Culture is continuous with Nature—continuous, in fact, with Creation: how language itself, as an inspired embodiment of culture, is deep and numinous. In "The Haunted Ruin," for example, he posits the continuity of biology and technology; how the warmth of the human hand enters the plastic of the computer keyboard, how the circuitry of microchip and coded information are continuous with blood and history:

Even your computer is a haunted ruin, as your
Blood leaves something of itself, warming
The tool in your hand.

From far off, down the billion corridors
Of the semiconductor, military
Pipes grieve at the junctures.

This too smells of the body, its heated
Polymers smell of breast milk
And worry-sweat.

Hum of so many cycles in current, voltage
Of the past. Sing, wires. Feel, hand. Eyes,
Watch and form

This effort to look everywhere, to survey and handle, is a central characteristic of Pinsky's ambition as a poet. The kaleidoscope of experience entrances him, and he wishes to render it and praise it, to invoke it and to provoke us to wonder. The drama of his stylistic transformation, from explainer to cantor, says something about the oddity and confidence of this poet. That lyric, shamanic impulse can be heard again in "Jersey Rain," which ends, "Original milk, replenisher of grief, / Descending destroyer, arrowed source of passion, / Silver and black, executioner, source of life." In moments like this, both ornamental and emotional, Pinsky has made himself a true anomaly: a modern poet of sacramental oratory.

Of the trio of poets discussed here, Pinsky is the one who has most declined ingratiation. That aesthetic choice—not to strive for intimacy with the reader—seems, in our compulsively friendly era, practically un-American. But Pinsky, the later Pinsky, conducts the poem not as a backstage exchange of confidences between equals, but as a dramatic performance. The reader is seated firmly in the audience. The God's-eye view in a poem like "The Figured Wheel" may not be affectionate, but what it offers instead is spectacle and sensation:

The figured wheel rolls through shopping malls and prisons,
Over farms, small and immense, and the rotten little
     downtowns.
Covered with symbols, it mills everything alive and grinds
The remains of the dead in the cemeteries, in unmarked
     graves and oceans.

Sluiced by salt water and fresh, by pure and contaminated rivers,
By snow and sand, it separates and recombines all droplets
     and grains,
Even the infinite sub-atomic particles crushed under the
     illustrated,
Varying treads of its wide circumferential track.

Spraying flecks of tar and molten rock it rumbles
Through the Antarctic station of American sailors and
     technicians,
And shakes the floors and windows of whorehouses for
     diggers and smelters

From Bethany, Pennsylvania to a practically nameless,
   semi-penal New Town

In the mineral-rich tundra of the Soviet northernmost
   settlements.

In an age that mistrusts language as never before, in which many poets
take the inadequacy of speech as a central preoccupation, Pinsky is
a rarity, the contemporary poet who has found language adequate,
fruitful, and enlivening. For him the activity of naming is both sacred
and pleasurable, numinous as anything else in creation. Those who
see Pinsky as bookish or academic are mistaken; it is more true to say
that he is an avid polyglot, who loves to fuse different materials and
styles into his music. In the poem "Avenue," he chants a catalogue of
streetlife, both its denizens and their lingos. Listen to how the prosaic
intensifies into a baroque jargonistic music:

   They persist. The jobber tells
The teller in the bank and she retells

Whatever it is to the shopper and the shopper
Mentions it to the retailer by the way.
They mutter and stumble, derelict. They write
These theys I write. Scant storefront pushbroom Jesus

Of Haitian hardware—they travel in shadows, they flog
Sephardic softgoods. They strain. Mid-hustle they faint
And shrivel. Or snoring on grates they rise to thrive.
Bonemen and pumpkins of All Saints. Kol Nidre,

Blunt shovel of atonement, a blade of song
From the terra-cotta temple: Lord, forgive us
Our promises, we chant. Or we churn our wino
Syllables and stares on the Avenue.

In such thrusting, variegated textures, one can hear the descriptive litany permutate into a kind of ecstatic stream of conscious-

ness. In such driving, stylized catalogues, we find as precedent not
Walt Whitman, but Gerard Manley Hopkins, whose language simi-
larly strains to swallow the world, to be both narrative and oratorio.
Hopkins's "Pied Beauty" is also a feverish litany, praising God for:

> Landscape plotted and pierced—fold, fallow, and plough;
>   And all trades, their gear and tackle and trim.
>
> All things counter, original, spare, strange;
>   Whatever is fickle, freckled (who knows how?)
>   With swift, slow; sweet, sour; adazzle, dim;
> He fathers-forth whose beauty is past change:
>   Praise him.

One considers the rich body of Pinsky's work with respect, admiration, even exhilaration; even so, there can be an imperviousness
about its performances that keeps us out, and instinctively perhaps,
we retain our own reserve. Yet in American poetry he is unique.
Where Hass finds emotional refuge in the world of nature, and Glück
lodges her sense of self within the logical citadels of self-argument,
Pinsky may be the widest-ranging in his celebration of life; he roams
through the realms of data and modernity, multiculturalism and technology and artifact, with gusto and appetite. He has an uncommon,
uncontemporary enthusiasm for the created. For all his cultural acumen, his stance is not judgmental but appreciative.

Pinsky can still be seen as a poet trying to balance comprehensiveness with compression, intellectual reach with accessibility. In the recent work, many poems seem to have adjusted themselves into the
mode of the ode, a song of praise in which resourcefulness, not closure or persuasion, is important. The form may be traditional, but
the objects of his praise are often unexpected. Here is a passage from
"To Television."

> Terrarium of dreams and wonders.
> Coffer of shades, ordained
> Cotillion of phosphors
> Or liquid crystal

Homey miracle, tub
Of acquiescence, vein of defiance.
Your patron in the pantheon would be Hermes

Raster dance,
Quick one, little thief, escort
Of the dying and comfort of the sick,

In a blue glow my father and little sister sat
Snuggled in one chair watching you
Their wife and mother was sick in the head
I scorned you and them as I scorned so much

This shows something, perhaps, of how Pinsky has deployed his intellectual and verbal facility: to venerate a popular cultural experience despised by high culture, employing a language that is itself complex and variably elevated, but not exactly academic. "Vein of defiance"? What that means, I haven't a clue. But "little thief, escort / Of the dying" is beautiful, exact, complex in resonance, and bold. Pinsky the mature poet seems willing to be difficult, or even intermittently obscure, for the sake of his cobbled poem. At the same time, the brief personal story of the fourth stanza above also shows how well Pinsky understands the necessary counterpoint of high and low, the shiny filigreed and the warmly homespun. Most of his poems wisely make a point, like this, of quilting a narrative window into their lapidary surfaces. Likewise in his audacious "Ode to Meaning," he free-associates on meaning itself:

Untrusting I court you. Wavering
I seek your face, I read
That Crusoe's knife
Reeked of you, that to defile you
The soldier makes the rabbi spit on the torah.
"I'll drown my book," says Shakespeare.

but later in the poem arrives at the passionate declaration:

Absence,
Or presence ever at play:
Let those scorn you who never
Starved in your dearth. If I
Dare to disparage
Your harp of shadows I taste
Wormwood and motor oil, I pour
Ashes on my head. You are the wound. You
Be the medicine.

Biblical, ornate, and passionate, at once old and new; this is unlike anything else contemporary.

Truly, Pinsky seems to have invented his own form and style in this confident shamanic eccentricity, something fashioned from the past and the present, a poetry both sound- and intellect-intensive. These poems accommodate feeling and intellect, they survey the human enterprise, they almost always touch on (like Milosz, another notable influence) the history of human consciousness and its place in nature. His rhetorical capacity and cultural acumen make Pinsky better suited than almost anyone to represent the postmodern situation— its wonders, duplicities, and estrangements. From the start of his career, in various ways, he has been thinking creatively for the We. In his muscular, inventive way, he could go in any direction.

Robert Hass: History and the Smell of Eucalyptus

Like Robert Pinsky, Robert Hass has been a restless, ambitious artist. Both poets have an encyclopedic bent and the modernist desire to pull the whole spectrum of the world into their field of vision. Where Pinsky has focused on the glories of the man-made—Culture—Hass has aimed much of his attention at exploring the dialectical echoes between the natural and the human. Where Pinsky's nature is to be more rhetorically willful (consider a poem like "Samurai Song" or "The Figured Wheel"), Hass might be described as a speculative describer who has made a tender tentativeness part of his style. Even moving through his own mind, it seems, he has the delicacy of an

ecologist who wants to record an environment without disturbing
a leaf. At the same time that Hass is tonally tentative, he is also re-
sourcefully inquisitive, ever probing into other sources and pockets of
consideration. It is the paradoxical blend of these qualities—gentility
combined with a probing persistence—that best describes his poetics. His ability to register and collate the subtleties of subjective and
objective experience is exceptional.

Above everything, Hass's work is stamped by its fluent, disarm-
ing naturalness of voice. Were it not for this amazing on-the-page
naturalness of affect, Hass might have been a scholar-poet; he has
something of the disposition for it, the all-you-can-eat appetite for
learning and cross-referencing. He can discuss T'ang statuary and
Heidegger in such a way as to make a reader feel both intrigued and
qualified to listen.

Unmistakably, Hass belongs to the narrative-meditative tradition, its
mellow humanist tutorials. Yet several things complicate his relation to
that tradition. One is a deep postmodern mistrust of the easy manners
of wisdom. The other is an ongoing and related dissatisfaction with closure. Almost from the start, he has insistently, restlessly monkeyed with
conventions of form. On the one hand, Hass yearns for the luminous,
one-stroke simplicity of haiku; on the other, a form so inclusive it never
resolves. In his shape-shifting career, he has attempted both.

Even in his first book, *Field Guide* (1973), Hass was experimenting
with form as a method to accommodate inclusiveness and his sense
of manifold existences. The early poem "Maps," for instance, is an as-
semblage in which the units are individual examples of what can constitute a map—at the same time, they make a sort of impressionistic
collage of California history. Here are seven sections of the thirteen-
section poem:

Sourdough french bread and pinot chardonnay
   *

Apricots—
the downy buttock shape
hard black sculpture of the limbs
on Saratoga hillsides in the rain.
    *

These were the staples of the China trade:
sea otter, sandalwood, and bêche-de-mer

     *

The pointillist look of laurels
their dappled pale green body stirs
down valley in the morning wind
Daphne was supple
my wife is tan, blue-rippled
pale in the dark hollows

     *

....

The night they bombed Hanoi
we had been drinking red pinot
that was winter the walnut tree was bare
and the desert ironwood where waxwings
perched in spring drunk on pyracantha

squalls headwinds days gone
north on the infelicitous Pacific

     *

....

Chants, recitations:
Olema
Tamalpais Mariposa
Mendocino Sausalito San Rafael
Emigrant Gap
Donner Pass

Of all the laws
that bind us to the past
the names of things are
stubbornest

     *

....

The long ripple in the swamp grass
is a skunk
he shuns the day

"Maps" might be called a constellation poem, and even thirty years after it was written, in form and content it tells a good deal about Hass's sensibility. The poem employs an engaged kind of sampling, whose elements create a field both particular and open, a sort of drifting enclosure. "Maps" is a collage of cultural history, descriptive naturalism, and sometimes, more rarely, fragments of personal information. The materials are alternately sensuous, factual, and intellectual. The ambient emotional mood is—again, typical of this poet—understated grief, wonder, curiosity, sometimes wry self-commentary. The art is in the arrangement of scale and variety. That the poem has no dominant emphasis nor evident narrator is significant: many points but no nucleus. Hass may be the contemporary master of the synthetic collage.

One notices, for all its range and delicacy, the reticence of such a poem—how little open assertiveness it possesses. In a much later poem, Hass cites Mallarmé on the subject of music: "the great thing is that it can resolve an argument / without ever stating the terms." One senses that Hass, too, would like to avoid the regrettable crudity of being explicit; he would rather endlessly infer.

Louise Glück, in her essay on Hass—fiercely barbed but typically keen—makes various telling complaints:

> Hass characteristically resists resolution: a mark of intellect,
> but also a temperamental inclination which can create its own
> form of stasis, in that it lacks not motion but momentum. . . .
> Hass may assert the fact of limitation, but limitation does not
> seem to be an attribute of the voice. . . . His poems are, regu-
> larly, a flight from self; what they lack, when they lack any-
> thing, is a sense of the restrictions of self, of singleness, which
> perception necessitates acts of judgment, decision, assertion
> of priorities. His poems repudiate self in its
> romantic role: bedrock, shaping principle.

Glück's comments, naturally, say a great deal about her poetics. Her own poems are so urgently about fixing the position of the self, deducing and declaring the laws that bind it, that the extreme fluidity of a poet like Hass makes her suspicious. To an artist of Glück's prosecutorial temperament, a poet like Hass is a dreamy relativist who will not seize and strike a stance, and thus cannot achieve the crucifying dramatic force Glück prefers in poetry.

Yet even discounting such prejudices, Glück gets much right: elusiveness and deflection are part of Hass's preferred operating mode. Though temperamentally romantic, Hass shows a deep reluctance about using selfhood as a fixed poetic center, and this has played a large role in his poetic destiny. Like those other ecological-Californian poets, Gary Snyder and Kenneth Rexroth, who know their place in nature, Hass doesn't consider the self a discrete, isolated thing. It makes perfect sense that he (again, like those other poets) would have translated the minimal, wry Chinese poets and that references to Buddhism would recur in his poems ("Bashō said: avoid adjectives of scale, you will love the world more and desire it less"). The mildly self-effacing beginning of "Spring Drawing" (whose title itself is "Eastern") exemplifies the poet's manners of artistic modesty, plus the implied inadequacy of the whole writing endeavor:

> A man thinks *lilacs against white houses,* having seen them in
>   the farm country south of Tacoma in April, and can't find
>   his way to the end of a sentence,

Likewise, the opening of Hass's well-known "Meditation at Lagunitas" suggests the poet's skepticism about human originality, implicitly including his own.

> All the new thinking is about loss.
> In this it resembles all the old thinking.

Hass's brilliance is the subtlety and insight with which he gathers and blends perception and cognition, the natural and the social, the sensuous and intellectual. He has devised for himself, and learned to inhabit, a kind of poem that is decentered and nonlinear, rhythmic and intuitive, one that, like Wordsworth's, can incorporate and digest its own doubts and feelings as it goes along, without requiring that they be brought to crisis. The classic Hass poem spirals in and out. In a word, Hass strives for an "organic" poetics, a mode of sensibility, not persuasion. In one of his poetical statements, he speaks admiringly of Chinese poems that "open themselves with such clarity of mind and such freedom from prehensile, conceptual imposition . . . that they . . . make an entire reality." What a perfect echo of Keats's statement on negative capability. Unmistakably this description represents an aspect of his own aspiration. Here is an excerpt from the title poem in *Human Wishes:*

> This morning the sun rose over the garden wall and a rare blue sky leaped from east to west. Man is altogether desire, say the Upanishads. Worth anything, a blue sky, says Mr. Acker, the Shelford gardener. Not altogether. In the end. Last night on television the ethnologist and the cameraman watched with hushed wonder while the chimpanzee carefully stripped a willow branch and inserted it into the anthill. He desired red ants. When they crawled slowly up the branch, he ate them, pinched between long fingers as the zoom lens enlarged his face. Sometimes he stopped to examine one, as if he were a judge at an ant beauty contest or God puzzled suddenly by the idea of suffering. There was an empty place in the universe where that branch wasn't and the chimp filled it, as Earlene, finding no back on an old Welsh cupboard she had bought in Saffron Walden, imagined one there and . . . went into town looking for a few boards of eighteenth-century tongue-and-groove pine

It's all here—the richness of association, the subtle elevation and demotion of subject matter and selves, the elusive marginality of the narrator, the "refusal of singleness" that Glück dislikes, the conceptual rhyme, the steady displacement of one thing after another. At his best, as this suggests, we are carried along on something that feels like perfect thought. This kind of magic is all the more impressive for the continual unpretentiousness of tone, the diffusing of self-congratulations, and the extraordinary layerings of sensibility as realm after realm is admitted into the poem.

Hass's themes, roughly summarized, are the coexistence of beauty and suffering, pleasure and pain: history and the smell of eucalyptus. His poetic temptations arise from the very amplitude of his temperament: shapelessness, plus a tendency toward the sentimental. Sometimes the poems are so opposed to closure, so rich and ambient, that they seem to lack decisiveness of structure. Like a highly conscious fog, the poem spills from one remarkable cupped moment or insight into the next, without letting any point intensify into judgment.

This occasional softness is a corollary of the desire to be holistic. At the same time, Hass's sensibility has a moral streak—he feels the need to make commitments, not just explanations. Like Glück, almost despite himself, Hass well knows that poems are persuasions, advocating judgment. But the decisive, satisfying force of moralizing is forbidden to Hass, by both his civility and by the breadth of his understanding.

If one cared to get psychological, one might hypothesize reasons for Hass's elusiveness. Hass is of the generation of American men—the 1960s, Vietnam era—who, because of their misgivings about power and patriarchy, renounced certain kinds of authority. Perhaps as a result, a refusal of overt assertiveness is inscribed in his poetics. Glück and Pinsky, in their distinct ways, are both oracular, but Hass wants little to do with final judgments. In a Hass poem, the speaker is always skirting the stage—rarely standing in its center. Hass would rather be, as the beginning of "Spring Drawing" suggests, a scribe than an oracle, and when you look at the palette of his emotions—wonder, curiosity, grief, nostalgia, insight—you find all the tender-hearted sensitivities, but not much anger. Even irony, in Hass, is always converted into something less toxic, less menacing— bemused regret or mournful wonder.

The risk that naturally accompanies so much empathy is sentimentality—which may be Hass's biggest poetic shadow. When he sometimes evokes an emotional solution to a complex dialectical poem, one feels that it reflects his desire to leap from Knowing into Being, from the claustrophobic confinement of the intellect into the sensual and ecstatic. One such moment concludes "Interrupted Meditation," from *Sun Under Wood,* a moment that seems suspiciously sweet:

> I know we die,
> and don't know what is at the end. We don't behave well.
> And there are monsters out there, and millions of others

to carry out their orders. We live half our lives
in fantasy, and words. This morning I am pretending
to be walking down the mountain in the heat.
A vault of blue sky, traildust, the sweet medicinal
scent of mountain grasses, and at trailside—
I'm a little ashamed that I want to end this poem
singing, but I want to end this poem singing—the wooly
closed-down buds of the sunflower to which, in English,
someone gave the name, sometime, of pearly everlasting.

Hass is such a generous, talented writer, capable at time of such tough observation, that this resolution seems slightly saccharine. Even here, though, the ambition is large: to set in poetic equilibrium the eternity of the privileged sensuous moment with the presence of history; acknowledging both, excluding neither.

What Hass says of the Swedish poet Tomas Tranströmer applies equally well to himself: "The style is, simply, the attentive, loose wandering of *Baltics*, a sort of slowly turning mobile of mind . . . in which discourse occurs because the separate parts tug at one another and everything seems metaphorically related." For Hass, Tranströmer's long poem resolves itself, if it does, purely through a key, unifying figure in the final section. One of Hass's most triumphant recent poems, "Dragonflies Mating," likewise ends in a figure that lends shape to the whole poem:

This morning in the early sun,
steam rising from the pond the color of smoky topaz,
a pair of delicate copper-red, needle-fine insects
are mating in the unopened crown of a Shasta daisy
just outside your door. The green flowerheads look like
    wombs
or the upright, supplicant bulbs of a vegetal pre-erection.
The insect lovers seem to be transferring the cosmos into
    each other
by attaching at the tail, holding utterly still, and quivering
    intently.

I think (on what evidence?) that they are different from us.
That they mate and are done with mating.
They don't carry all this half-mated longing up out of childhood
and then go looking for it everywhere.
And so, I think, they can't wound each other the way we do.
They don't go through life dizzy or groggy with their hunger,
kill with it, smear it on everything,
. . . .
My insect instructors have stilled, they are probably stuck
    together
in some bliss and minute pulse of after-longing
evolution worked out to suck the last juice of the world
into the receiver body. They can't separate probably
until it is done.

Anyone, I think, can recognize that this is extraordinary writing, but in order to appreciate the rippling resonance of this figure, a reader has to know that the full poem recounts creation stories of California Indians and his own haunted disdainful relationship with his alcoholic mother—as well as ten other things. Hass perceives the world as so stuck together, it can't be unstuck: out of this adhesion comes the poetry. In an ending like this, he achieves a symphonic resolution without ever sacrificing his receptivity. Without appearing to strain, he thinks deep and long; without appearing to assert, he suggests important moral probabilities. In his best poems, as here, he achieves power without appearing ever to have seized it. The kind of struggling elegance visible in this passage embodies a kind of radiant moral sentience few contemporaries can equal.

In Hass's career, there is no clear turn in the road, no obvious crisis and redeployment. Rather, it has been a continuous wrestling, a fretful seeking for representations of experience that do not oversimplify for the sake of poetic force or mere resolution. In recent work, he has shown an interesting willingness to be more linguistically baroque, less "natural," and this might make for interesting future developments. Four or five elaborate, multisectioned and multistyled poems have anchored his most recent book, suggesting the poet's craving for even more tentacled, polyvalent forms. Without doubt such formal experiments will continue.

Louise Glück: The Legends Cannot Be Trusted

The poems of Louise Glück make a radical contrast to those of Pinsky and Hass. In contrast to their sprawling freedoms, Glück's poems are relatively short and remarkable for their psychic density and concentration. Her working vocabulary is likewise highly economical, and her obsessions are more immediately identifiable—usually they enact the internal argument of a speaker in crisis. The nature of Glück's talent is resoundingly dramatic, distinctly different from the more discursive male laureates. Yet it could be said that she has farmed a narrow patch of land as productively as they have shopped the whole world. Her worldview, in contrast to theirs, is tragic. (Hass is sad, not tragic; Pinsky is triumphant)

For Hass and Pinsky, expansiveness has been both burden and joy, but Glück is essentially a narrowing poet. In Glück's work, the radiance and gravity of the poems grow out of the enormous pressure exerted on the contents of a small container. The volcanic world of feeling, channeled into strict forms determined by rhetoric and logic, creates a poetic experience of confrontation and breakthrough, in which the self triumphs even while losing. This scenario is well represented by the title poem in her 1985 collection, *The Triumph of Achilles.* The poem retells the Homeric story of Achilles and Patroclus, and, as so often in Glück's work, leads us to see how the bond of love is a fatal, contaminating one when it comes to the freedom of the self:

> In the story of Patroclus
> no one survives, not even Achilles
> who was nearly a god.
> Patroclus resembled him; they wore
> the same armor.
>
> Always in these friendships
> one serves the other, one is less than the other:
> the hierarchy
> is always apparent, though the legends
> cannot be trusted—
> their source is the survivor,
> the one who has been abandoned.

What were the Greek ships on fire
Compared to this loss?

In his tent, Achilles
grieved with his whole being
and the gods saw

he was a man already dead, a victim
of the part that loved,
the part that was mortal.

In this imperial authorial tone, and plain, relentless language, Glück issues forth her truth-statements with prosecutorial logic; what they organize is an intertwining deductive sequence of propositions and conclusions that go something like this:

Proposition A.   Humanness is defined by the ability to love.
Proposition B.   The object of human love will die.
Proposition C.   The survivor, not the deceased, is the
                 unfortunate one.

   Corollary: To survive is to be abandoned.
   Corollary: The one who dies is the lucky one.
   Corollary: Not to love would be god-like.
   Corollary: To love is to die.

What we feel, in reading such sequences, is partly the thrill of absolutism, and partly the exultation one experiences in the presence of clarity. Chilling and intoxicating, Glück's assertiveness wouldn't work if she were not a master of the paradox, of polarizing the deep contradictoriness in experience. For, though they appear ruthlessly truthful, direct as a sequence of hammer blows, the poems are often enough (not always) the perverse logic of a damaged speaker. As the speaker of the Achilles poem says, "the legends / cannot be trusted." In both tone and content, Glück's poems are layered with cunning strategies and subtexts. Consider, for instance, the way that one crucial premise is smuggled into the modifying appositive clause, "the one who has been abandoned." These logical structures always intensify the force of the poem; often they also enrich the intellectual-emotional world of the poem. "The Triumph of Achilles," for example, contains a rich subplot of inequality in friendship: "Always (. . .) / one serves the other." That plot is not *obviously* integral to the main thrust of the poem (i.e., to love is to die), yet tangled beneath the surface, it troubles and haunts us with a whole secondary set of insinuations.

Glück's early gift was the strident striking of postures—like talented actors (as the term dramatic monologue suggests), the speakers take impressively ferocious stances. To demonstrate the deep consistency of Glück's early and even middle work, and its potential for poetic stagnancy as well, we can look at "Love Poem" from *The House on Marshland*, 1975, a poem that works the same deadly syllogistic logic practiced in "Triumph of Achilles":

Love Poem

> There is always something to be made of pain.
> Your mother knits.
> She turns out scarves in every shade of red.
> They were for Christmas, and they kept you warm
> while she married over and over, taking you
> along. How could it work,
> when all those years she stored her widowed heart
> as though the dead come back.
> No wonder you are the way you are,
> afraid of blood, your women
> like one brick wall after another.

The theme of the ironically titled "Love Poem" might be paraphrased like this: what keeps you warm will ruin you for life. As in the Achilles poem, the part of the self attached to another is portrayed as a crippling deficit. Though the means of "Love Poem" are somewhat plainer and less fluent than the later poem, the message is very consonant. Here, too, one admires the way the poem is complexly "stacked": the way the mother and son are both "in storage," for example. Again the syllogistic sequence: A is true and B is true and therefore, C is bad news. Intentionally or not, those who love you will destroy your autonomy. Partialness of character dictates a self-fulfilling fate. Like so many Glück poems, "Love Poem" has the flavor of a customer complaint, an accusation against life.

After her first four books, an onlooker might have guessed that Glück was set up for a strong but repetitive career. Her theme seemed monologically fixed upon the dark dilemmas of wounded character and fate. Insight, though it could not heal, offered the compensation of self-knowledge and clarity, cold contact with the facts. Her great gift was (and is) a fatalistic intensity, and her unique practice the peculiar coupling of a surgical rationality with passionate psychological insight; her poems unite the nobility of cognition with the pathos of suffering. But the voice of her interrogations—absolutist, dramatic, fatalistic—seemed locked, and the field of her poems, for all the intelligence and intensity, seemed narrow.

Yet Glück's development in the next three books—*Ararat, The Wild Iris,* and *Meadowlands*—is one of the great examples of redeployment in our time. Her ability to diagnose and reconfigure her own poetic strategies has been nothing less than amazing. This developmental triumph was not inevitable. Not only has the poet repeatedly discovered different dramatic structures, she also discovered whole new octaves of tone.

It was in *Ararat,* her fifth book, published in 1990, that Glück let go of the strict, strident tone that had been so effective for her. The *Ararat* poems, like the earlier work, still circulate around autobiographical myths of family and still orchestrate paradoxical truths, but the tone had softened, from one of imperious justice-seeking to a more relaxed, retrospective wonder. Tonally the poetry moved from grievance to grief. In the earlier poetry, Glück's use of narrative detail is largely intellectual prop, furniture for the stagehands of logic to move around. But the anecdotes in *Ararat,* though they still exude the aura of parable, are not just visual aids for the exposition of principles. Compared to the curt telling of "Love Story," for example, the entry into "Terminal Resemblance" seems like leisurely storytelling:

> When I saw my father for the last time, we both did the same
>   thing.

He was standing in the doorway to the living room,
waiting for me to get off the telephone.
That he wasn't also pointing to his watch
was a signal he wanted to talk.

Talk for us always meant the same thing.
He'd say a few words. I'd say a few back.
That was about it.

It was the end of August, very hot, very humid.
Next door, workmen dumped new gravel on the driveway.

My father and I avoided being alone;
we didn't know how to connect, to make small talk—
there didn't seem to be
any other possibilities.

The risk Glück ran in writing *Ararat* in such plain style was drabness; in de-escalating her drama from the level of crisis, she took the chance of becoming prosaic, of writing at less than primary dramatic force. Yet one can see that this loosening was crucial and rewarding. The decrease in stridency allowed the entire poetic means, from tone to structure, to ease and shift.

In *Ararat*, Glück also chose a project relaxed enough to interrogate her own motive and method. Never entirely unconscious of the ironies of her particular vision ("such a mistake to want / clarity above all things," she says in one poem), in *Ararat*, the paradox of certainty achieved at the cost of estrangement is moved sometimes to center stage. The legitimacy of her own tragic vision is regularly deconstructed. In the poem "Widows," for example, she says of a card game: "that's the object: in the end, / the one who has nothing wins." Despite the oracular delivery, the love of ultimate conclusions, the speakers in *Ararat* regularly acknowledge their complicity in the construction of the stage; nowhere perhaps so definitively as in "The Untrustworthy Speaker," excerpted here.

Don't listen to me; my heart's been broken.
I don't see anything objectively.

. . . .

When I speak passionately,
that's when I'm least to be trusted.

It's very sad, really: all my life, I've been praised
for my intelligence, my powers of language, of insight.
In the end, they're wasted—
. . . .
That's why I'm not to be trusted.
Because a wound to the heart
is also a wound to the mind.

"The Untrustworthy Speaker" is a striking demonstration of how, through self-consciousness, the maturing poet could enlarge and complicate the playing field of her poems. Glück's previous work had come from establishing a limited point of view and rendering its consequences in the most absolute terms. In *Ararat* the scope of inquiry significantly widened.

If *Ararat* presented a new, less punishing mode of self-examination, *Wild Iris* was a major strategic redeployment, a brilliant solution to the problem of Glück's poetics of fortress-like singularity. In many ways, the psychological and poetic impasses in Glück's work were identical: how to escape the limits of perspective of a self whose character is stamped. In *Wild Iris,* Glück's book of Genesis, the poet divides her consciousness and speaker's voice among three viewpoints: God, Flowers, Human. What this strategy of ventriloquism allowed Glück, most profoundly, was a liberation from the singular locked perspective of the sufferer. Though the *Wild Iris* poems are monologues, they are in dialogue with one another. To imaginatively inhabit the simple but profound perspective of flowers, and the voice of an all-knowing creator seemed to provide Glück the writer access to the backstory of The Fall. In "Sunset," an address hypothetically cast in the voice of God-to-human, the issues and the irony are familiar— but the perspective is unprecedented in the poet's work:

My great happiness
is the sound your voice makes
calling to me even in despair; my sorrow

that I cannot answer you
in speech you accept as mine.

You have no faith in your own language.
So you invest
authority in signs
you cannot read with any accuracy.

Though this is still a story of tragic disconnection, the poem imaginatively transcends the condition of exile to an altitude of compassion, even—in a dark way—bemusement. Moreover, the poem identifies a collectively human condition, not just that of one unique speaker. Likewise, in "The Red Poppy," Glück's flower-speaker can say things her human speaker would never say:

The great thing
is not having
a mind. Feelings:
oh, I have those; they
govern me. I have
a lord in heaven
called the sun, and open
for him, showing him
the fire of my own heart,

The project of *Wild Iris*, as described, sounds preposterous, but it resulted in a remarkable book (for which the poet won the Pulitzer). More importantly, *Wild Iris* broke apart the puzzle pieces that Glück had spent decades clamping together into airtight legalistic arguments against God. The energy released is palpable in the invention and fresh insights of this ventriloqual suite.

Meadowlands, her next collection, provided even further surprises: an airy liberation of Glück's voice, using the techniques and strategies she had learned in the two preceding books. Again, the sentiments and issues are familiar—but the acrobatic freedom of perspective, the variety of diction in the poems, could not have been predicted. Sometimes in the space of a single stanza, the speaker's self is analyzed, sympathized with, and mocked. The poem "Midnight," for example, at once serious and playful, contains elements of comedy and self-parody that make the speaker's estrangement more convincingly poignant and personal than the earlier, more straight-faced Glück:

Speak to me, aching heart: what
ridiculous errand are you inventing for yourself
weeping in the dark garage
with your sack of garbage: it is not your job
to take out the garbage, it is your job
to empty the dishwasher. You are showing off again,
exactly as you did in childhood—where
is your sporting side, your famous
ironic detachment?

This is not just excoriating, it is full of flourish. The danger for Glück as a poet has always been, and continues to be, barrenness of texture, a sort of aridity of argument. When her poems are less successful, it is because they consist sheerly of theses, without the augmenting joys of imagination. In the tonal bravado of *Meadowlands*, and since, Glück's work continues to sustain its high standards of intensity, both intellectual and passionate. No one sings the song of intoxicated singularity of consciousness like her or better gives voice to the most fundamental fractures of human nature. Her mid-career transformations are a testament to the resource of strategic intelligence.

"Profession" has always seemed like a misleading, even laughable word for poetry—not just because it suggests that the economy has a Poetry Sector, but also because it suggests that poetry is masterable, that poetry itself is stable, that some persons possess poetry, and that others don't. Though a skilled craftsperson can create a facsimile of a real poem, a skilled reader can spot the counterfeit in a minute, and the word that reader might use to describe the counterfeit might be "professional." The making of poems is so mysteriously tied up with not-knowing that in some sense the poet is a perpetual amateur, a stranger to the art, subject to ineptitude, failure, falsity, mediocrity, and repetitiveness. Even to remember what a poem IS seems impossible for a poet—one suspects that professors, or professionals, rarely have that problem.

Nonetheless, some poets, like those discussed here, make you want to use the word *professional* because their careers are testaments to their stamina of craft and spirit. Having found an initial place for themselves to stand and a way to speak, they have lost and found it again and again: they have reconceived themselves, gone past their old answers into the new questions. This combination of restlessness and intensity seems fundamental to the path of poetry. And because they have impressed us many times in the past, we follow along, knowing that on a given occasion in the future, unpredictably, they will knock the hats off our heads all over again—as if to remind us what we are in the presence of.

Self-Consciousness

Unlike riding a bike, with poetry,
you never quite know how.
—PHOEBE MILLIKIN

The gradual intrusion of self-consciousness is one inevitable side effect of an education in art. To read ten poems, or a hundred, is one thing. To read ten thousand is another. As we internalize more of the tradition and become progressively less shielded by our ignorance, we realize how local our upbringing has been, how much there might be to know, and perhaps even, sigh, how limited our talent. T. S. Eliot's Prufrock comes to know that he is not Prince Hamlet; we must deal with the fact that we are not Eliot. When a person takes the step toward learning more of craft and its history, more of artifice—when, for example, a person crosses the threshold of an MFA program—she chooses to end a childhood in artlessness. She gives up some of the innocent infatuation, the naïveté, the adolescent grandiosity, maybe even some of the natural grace of the beginner. "They are good poets because they don't know yet how hard it is to write a poem," I have heard a teacher say, a bit tartly, of her beginning poetry class.

This initiation into knowledge will infect the learner with the virus of self-consciousness. As a consequence of learning of the existence of the poems of W. H. Auden, or Marianne Moore, or Louise Glück, your writing may suddenly seem horribly simplistic, crude as crayon drawings on Masonite. Now the poem, even as you are making it, seems stiff, clumsy, and obvious. Now your work may become, in compensation, coy and encoded.

Yet that very knowledge, which can inhibit and choke, can also inspire and challenge. Self-consciousness is the necessary border crossing of craft, skill, and even of poetic ambition. Each of the following examples are visibly aware of, and creatively askew from, poetic normalities:

> . . . The roses
> Had the look of flowers that are looked at.
> (FROM "BURNT NORTON," T. S. ELIOT)

> We were walking under some big trees—trees, you know what
>   they look like.
> (MARK FRANCONATTI)

> I know that John Clare's madness nature could not straighten.
> (JON ANDERSON)

> Look stranger, on this island now
> The leaping light for your delight discovers,
> (W. H. AUDEN)

Self-consciousness in writing, as it does in life, opens up a kind of delay between impulse and action, between thought and word. That pause—as these examples show—offers the opportunity for calculated intensifications and angularities that would never occur in "natural," uninformed speech. Such special effects may be manifested in sound, as in Auden's exaggerated alliterations, or in image, like Eliot's cross-eyed figure for perceptual self-estrangement. Similarly, the awkward syntax of Jon Anderson's line recreates the psychological struggle it describes.

Such special effects can deepen the texture and register of a poem. So, one payoff for knowing conventions is the chance to redesign them, to invent the next generation of convention. In Cynthia Huntington's poem, "O California" the poet grafts unexpected subject matter to the lofty tone and syntax of invocation. Thus she pours new wine into old skins:

> Oh falling, sinking, sliding-over-rooftops
> moon of harvest orange, look down
> into white caverns of immaculate garages
> turned inside out by light, the glowing icicles,
> lawnmowers and shimmering grasses
> dewed by sprinklers whose iron blossoms
> rise from the ground to spurt
> and shower at our feet, oh moon, lean down
> and tell me the meaning of money.

Huntington uses the antique rhetorical convention of apostrophe in her invocation and address to the moon. This is a familiar enough poetic project: "Oh moon, look down and tell me!" But what the moon sees has changed into unpoetic North American suburban paraphernalia. And the unexpected noun-object this uncoiling sentence arrives at—money—ripples backward through the entire sentence, shocking the trope awake. The poet's savoir-faire has rescued us from an experience of aesthetic repetition and also achieved a tone both rapturous and ironic, self-mocking yet grave. Money is, as we are now led to recognize, a serious and mysterious subject. The poet has embedded new subject matter inside old poetic manners, and those manners have inherited force and shape. The rhythmic, syntactical momentum of the sentence gathers and drives its full force into the wedge of the final surprising word.

In other instances, awareness of the conventionality of certain subject matter necessitates a strategic approach to the topic. In Lawrence Ferlinghetti's poem "In Goya's Greatest Scenes We Seem to See . . . ," the speaker engineers an indirect route to his topic because the poem's theme—human misery—is a jaded and overfamiliar one. The poem begins by assuming the reassuringly civilized guise of a European art lecture:

In Goya's greatest scenes we seem to see
                              the people of the world
            exactly at the moment when
                  they first attained the title of
                                          'suffering humanity'
            They writhe upon the page
                              in a veritable rage
                                          of adversity
            Heaped up
                  groaning with babies and bayonets
                                    under cement skies
            in an abstract landscape of blasted trees
                  bent statues bats wings and beaks
                        slippery gibbets
                  cadavers and carnivorous cocks
                  and all the final hollering monsters
                  of the
                              'imagination of disaster'
                  they are so bloody real
                              it is as if they really still existed

And they do

            Only the landscape is changed
. . . .
They are the same people
                              only further from home
            on freeways fifty lanes wide
                  on a concrete continent
                              spaced with bland billboards
                  illustrating imbecile illusions of happiness

Ultimately, Ferlinghetti wishes to describe, and to indict, the dehumanized landscape of civilized man. But he is no naïve seventeen-year-old, caught up in the first flush of outrage and self-important righteousness: he wants to be passionate, but doesn't want to lapse into literary or political cliché. In order to make his drama compelling, he must escort the reader toward involvement by certain roundabout avenues.

This trip the reader goes on is a kind of disorientation and a kind of re-education. Posing as an art historian is one of the poet's many smart moves, but Ferlinghetti's most brilliant repositioning might be the speaker's ironic presentation of the phrase "suffering humanity" as if it were an exhausted advertising slogan. It is language, not humanity, that is initially held up for our inspection by quotation marks. Served up on the sardonic, distancing detachment of "they . . . attained the title," the poet simultaneously invites us to dismiss the suffering referred to, while calling our attention to the jaded vocabulary of its traditional publicity. In a moment, we recognize the worldliness of a speaker who has seen it all before, who resists sentiment and simplification. Consequently, we extend some of our trust to him.

Yet this initial stance of measured detachment is immediately undermined by the lurid, violently crude descriptions of medieval suffering that follow, that force us to re-encounter the meaning of that same exhausted phrase, "suffering humanity." The sequencing of the materials and the unfolding complexity of tone—from skepticism to sincerity, from knowing into feeling—gradually prepare us for the dramatic pivotal lines:

they are so bloody real
it is as if they still existed

And they do

The stage-by-stage progression of the discourse, from art history lecture to aghast spectatorship, from detachment to involvement, carries us along on its journey from the tragic past to an absurd modernity. The theme of suffering humanity is updated into its contemporary version, as is our faith in art's capacity to powerfully mirror life. Ferlinghetti's skillfully elliptical approach is an example of how self-consciousness, incorporated into a poem, can manage to freshly expose and penetrate a subject.

Both the Huntington and Ferlinghetti poems exhibit a knowledge of poetical history, language, and manners and deploy it with ingenuity. Ferlinghetti *has* to negotiate with his material in order to renew it. Huntington's more playful genetic engineering creates a poetical hybrid of old-high joined to low-new.

Maybe the vocabulary of genetics is an appropriate metaphor for this topic. Self-consciousness in art is a little like the use of radiation in laboratory experiments; while it can produce truly valuable genetic variants, it can just as easily lead to frightening mutations. Getting the dosage right is tricky. Holding a microscope up to language, to meaning itself, there is the danger of falling through, down into the infinite space between words.

The hinderedness of trying too hard, of watching yourself as you work, can afflict even a poet as masterful as Robert Hass. Look at the opening of his poem "Spring Drawing," a poem about the difficulty of writing:

A man thinks *lilacs against white houses,* having seen them in the farm country south of Tacoma in April, and can't find his way to a sentence, a brushstroke carrying the energy of *brush* and *stroke*

—as if he were stranded on the aureole of the memory of a woman's breast,

and she, after the drive from the airport and a chat with her mother and a shower, which is ritual cleansing and a passage through water to mark transition,

had walked up the mountain on a summer evening.

This brief excerpt provides instances of both the plus and minus of self-consciousness. In the first sentence, the speaker longs for the verbal naturalness of a brushstroke, "of *brush* and *stroke*." This deconstruction of both word and desire is clever, interesting, insightful, and to the point. Only an alert, sophisticated, and hard-working artist would have looked inside that compound word, considered the physical gesture it refers to, discovered the double nature of those noun-verbs. A moment like this, penetrating but not heavy-handed, is a good advertisement for savvy poetic intelligence.

But the next moment in the poem shows self-consciousness hyper-extended, entangled in a willfully ingenious simile. The writer-speaker describes his situation of impoverished imagination "*as if* he were stranded on the *aureole* of the *memory* of a woman's *breast*." This meta-double-decker image, meant to embody the main character's labored creative struggle, is clever but cumbersome, conceptually arduous, and unintentionally show-offy. It's not that hyperextension of metaphor is bad aesthetics, or that excessiveness of any kind is problematic, but this instance serves as an example of the overcalculated, the poet-who-knew-too-much.

Self-consciousness often provokes an overexertion of cleverness. But intelligence, when used well in a poem, never makes the reader feel less smart than the writer, or left behind. Rather, it gives the reader the exhilarating pleasure of being smart in concert *with* the speaker.

The goal of the healthy artist is not to be crippled by the weight of literacy, nor intimidated into a kind of aesthetic conservatism, nor to be engorged with fancy self-protective mannerisms, but to be selectively informed and empowered by knowledge. This development of sensibility could be called the acquisition and use of taste.

To learn what a poet needs to know is to become an initiate; that initiation imposes burdens as well as powers. We have the obligation to make real poems, to contribute to the living, evolving heritage of poetry. To make that contribution requires not just skill and desire, but a kind of discriminating insight into the deep structures of poetry. This resourcefulness surely must spring from the union of learning and bold inventiveness. Finally, if our awareness of the great Past makes us self-consciously anxious, it is good to remember that Everything has not been done. Possibility has not been exhausted. More reality is being made at the reality factory every day, and new ways to handle it are being invented—language is a technology, after all. Its adaptations are legion; its evolution is hardly over.

Two Roads Diverged

CHARACTER, METAPHOR, AND DESTINY
IN THE POEMS OF MATTHEWS AND LEVIS

In Chapter 13 of Raymond Chandler's novel *The Big Sleep*, Phillip Marlowe is being frisked by Eddie Mars's henchmen:

> *Eddie Mars said: "See if this bird is wearing any iron."*
> *The blond flicked a short-barreled gun out and stood pointing it at me. The pug sidled over flatfooted and felt my pockets with care. I turned around for him like a bored beauty modeling an evening gown.*

It's a typically brilliant Chandler image, and it illustrates the manifold and simultaneous functions of metaphor. To begin with, of course, the image presents action with a wonderful physical precision, enabling us to visualize the frisking. Secondly, the image is an elegant constituent of the speaker's voice: it characterizes our narrator, Philip Marlowe, as a nonchalant and ironic observer, coolheaded even when in apparent danger, distanced from the situation and himself.

These first two functions of Chandler's image could be called functions of Equivalency—they provide the reader with highly focused, real-world information relevant to the horizontal narrative. But a third dimension of Chandler's metaphor is that of the Fantastic, which is to say, the pure, dream-like fantasy of the image, uncalled-for and in-explicable, otherworldly in a way that has little or nothing to do with the situation or the plot of *The Big Sleep*. After all, the image isn't meant to suggest that Marlowe has a secret life as a drag queen. No, this fantastic aspect of metaphor is vertical, freestanding, and independent of the text; it exists for its own sake, an iconic delight, a quick trip to Hawaii in a city as cold as a set of brass knuckles.

Chandler's image illustrates the peculiar simultaneity of meta-phor, how surrealism and realism can coexist in a text without apparently creating a logical dilemma for the reader. Of course, in *The Big Sleep*, realism (or at least the noir fantasy of realism) is clearly the dominant paradigm. Chandler's wild metaphors exist as a kind of candy scattered on the narrative trail. At the same time, the rapture of these freestanding figures, which stud his tales, is an essential part of his style, and it seems the very embodiment of the pleasure principle.

Every mature writer has a highly evolved and individuated relationship with language, including metaphor. Like the use of a certain vocabulary ("the blond," "the pug sidled over"), or certain syntactical predilections, a writer's attitude toward metaphor is part of the DNA signature of style, a reflection of his or her personal temperament, a matter of nature, not nurture. Writers know that style is a thing worked out incrementally, over years of experiment and sequential influence, as a fusion of labor, craft, raw talent, instinct, and prevailing aesthetics. This working out of individual sensibility in the context of received cultural aesthetics is one of the fascinating dramas of literary studies.

In this essay I want to look at the evolution of metaphor in the work of two contemporary masters, William Matthews and Larry Levis. To study the use of metaphor in their work chronologically, and in juxtaposition, is to witness the process of poetic individuation. It is a story of both aesthetic history and temperament, and it illuminates the nature of metaphor itself.

Temperamentally, the two poets are very distinct from each other. Levis is an ecstatic poet of the dark romantic sort, whose relationship to image and metaphor is Dionysian. Matthews might be (somewhat reductively) described as a poet of classical temperament, interested finally in proportion, not exaggeration. But both poets came of artistic age in the early 1970s, when American surrealism was at its height, and when the image was the coin of the realm. As a consequence, their starting points in style are not so far apart as their natures would eventually take them.

In the late 1950s, '60s, and early '70s, the poetry of image and metaphor boomed in America, correspondent to the wholesale translation and importation of poetry from other countries. Translations of poets like Pablo Neruda, Cesar Vallejo, Federico García Lorca, and the French surrealists—poets who wrote in more radically imaginative modes than American poets—influenced American poetry tremendously. In effect, this poetry stimulated a counterrational revolution; the result was American surrealism. Poets like James Wright, Robert Bly, and W. S. Merwin were the pioneers of this paradigm shift. Younger poets as various as Bill Knott, Diane Wakowski, and Mark Strand were seeded in this aesthetic climate, in which the primacy of the image was essential. Levis and Matthews were also part of this generation.

William Matthews

The role of image in the work of William Matthews can be mapped from an early stage, when the image is a primary device, to a later stage in which the image is largely subordinated into the overall structure of a more highly textured poetry, one in which diction and syntax have more prominence than singular images.

Here, for example, is an early poem from Matthews's 1972 book, *Sleek for the Long Flight:*

Blues for John Coltrane, Dead at 41

Although my house floats on a lawn
as plush as a starlet's body
and my sons sleep easily,
I think of death's salmon breath

leaping back up the saxophone
with its wet kiss.

Hearing him dead,
I feel it in my feet
as if the house were rocked
by waves from a soundless speedboat
planing by, full throttle.

This work by the young poet, Matthews at twenty-eight, reflects
his lifelong preoccupation with jazz. But it also reflects the poetic climate of its time, when image was almost the only requirement for
being a poet, and when a poem could stand on the virtuosity of images alone. Image is certainly the principal device here, and we can
see that the images in "Blues" are somewhat surreal, even a little
show-offish in their vividness and disconnection. Why, for example,
is the lawn compared to a starlet's body? Yes, the image performs
what Bly would call a "leap," but is it a leap that transforms content?
Not really. In this poem, like a vivid jumble of colorful toys, we also
find the salmon of death, the river of the saxophone, a kissing fish,
and the dead Coltrane as a passing speedboat.

Skip forward seven years, to the 1979 book *Rising and Falling*, and
the beginning of the poem "The Icehouse, Pointe au Baril, Ontario,"
and we see an evident evolution in Matthews's temperament:

Each vast block in its batter
of sawdust must have weighed
as much as I did. The sweat
we gathered running down
the path began to glaze.
We could see our breaths,
like comic strip balloons
but ragged, grey, opaque.
. . . .
In the icehouse I'd clear my name
on a block of ice and the dank film
of sawdust on my finger was as dense

as parts of grown-up conversation,
the rivalry of uncles and managing
money. The managers I knew
wore baseball caps and yelled.
As for money, I thought it was like food.
When blueberries were in season
we ate them all the time.

Image still plays a major role in this later poem, but with some distinct differences from those we see in "Blues for John Coltrane, Dead at 41." The images in "The Icehouse, Pointe au Baril, Ontario" are markedly less surreal and more subordinated to narrative—a sign of Matthews's progress toward an aesthetic of coherence and comprehensiveness. He is no longer trading on what Mary Oliver calls the "jolting volts," the splash and zap of image. These images are less sensational and more devoted to a literal sensuousness. Analogously, a more sophisticated music is audible here: the wonderful webs of assonance inside "vast block in its batter / of sawdust" for example, or "must have weighed / as much as I did." Eventually Matthews would become our Mel Tormé, impeccable in phrasing and sound; that shift in the poet's attention, toward values of pure sound, away from the more visual aspect of pure image, is a spectral shift in aesthetic.

In content, too, the images in "Icehouse" suggest a redirection of Matthews's interests, toward a more analytical, even sociological perspective: the poem describes the shadowy, dawning awareness of civilization's discontents, "as dense / as parts of grown-up conversation," of the world beyond the self, of money and hierarchies of responsibility, and the difference between the worlds of grown-up and child ("As for money, I thought it was like food"). Yes, the poem is about the contrast between Innocence and Experience, but it also suggests the narrator's pleasurable anticipation of social complexity.

The increased sophistication and groundedness of "Icehouse," in contrast to "Blues," is emblematic of the poet that Matthews was becoming, a poet whose work ultimately would be about Consciousness rather than Unconsciousness. Not, in other words, a poet of the leaping explosive surprise of metaphor, but rather a discursive, descriptive, thinking-man's poet, one given to discriminating the fine gradients of experience.

Another ten years later, in the 1987 collection called *Foreseeable Futures,* the poem "Torch Song" shows the sonic fervor of the mature musician:

> From its shifting skin the bay had erased in turn
> the diligent scribbles of the lobster boats, the stitches
> tacking sailboats made, every glint and blur the sun
>
> had sown on the busy waters. The tide ran reticently
> out and chummily back in, and cormorants dove
> where herons had plied six hours earlier. At dusk,
>
> the wind stalled and the bay lay glassily bland.
> Later, moths convened on the bright windows like recurring
> dreams. Who will remember this unless it repeat itself?
>
> Weren't melons sapid and berries taut with sugar?
> Didn't the spirit wisp smokily from the rose-gray
> embers of the sleeping body?

In this poem Matthews's language has become even more densely textured. Figurative language is plentiful (*skin, erased, scribbles, stitches, reticent, plied*), but the linguistic priority embodied here is that of continuous sound and continuous inflection. Diction is so emphatically operative here that it suppresses metaphor as a distinct function; and though there are some metaphor-nouns here, most of the metaphors are in less prominent grammatical positions of verb, adverb, adjective. The imagery is embedded and submerged rather than iconic.

As Matthews turned his attention toward the sophisticated realm of diction and etymology, he gradually reduced his reliance on the singular, attention-grabbing metaphor. Ideologically, also, Matthews is finally a poet of perspective rather than epiphany; ultimately, he was pursuing integration, not Romantic transport. Like the classical poets Horace and Martial, whose work he loved and translated,

Matthews's work is finally stoical and humanist, which is to say, dedicated to finding and defining Balance: the reconciliation of pleasure with loss, of the individual with society, and of feeling with mind. His voice reaches to establish not otherness but commonality. Like Auden, with his great intelligence and erudition Matthews elected to be a citizen of culture: critiquing it, praising it, defining its values and failures. To such a discursive, civilizing temperament, the use of metaphor in its fantastic, iconic function may have come to seem something of a distraction. What is clear is that as Matthews the discursive musician evolved, sensational freestanding metaphors lost their appeal for him.

Larry Levis

It is a different story, and a different journey, for Larry Levis, a poet who sustained his interest in ecstatic vision to the end. Like Matthews, Levis came of age in the early 1970s, in the climate of American surrealism, but for him it was a lifelong temperamental alliance. The main talent of his first book was the one required by the era: oddity of image. Here is "Applause" a small poem from *Wrecking Crew*, published in 1972.

> These wings buried beneath a thin cocoon
> struggle quietly and open
> just as people begin applauding over
> by the bandstand.
> > I feel like a
> moth on the lip of a waterfall.

How tame this poem seems in comparison with Levis's later poems! What a modest irrationality! And retrospectively, it seems very 1960s, creating as it does a mildly surreal equivalence between a hatching moth and the speaker's own inward sense of blossoming to a strange marvelous world.

William Matthews's vision is finally a social one, and he uses metaphor largely to illuminate the outer, collective world through his sensibility, but even in a slight poem like "Applause," Levis manifests the deep-image emphasis on inwardness. In that sense, Levis resides closer to the vision for art embodied and articulated by the surrealists: the primary values are imagination, discovery, and surprise.

Five years later, in 1977, Levis's second and decidedly most surreal book, *The Afterlife,* presents a far more radical relation to image. Levis had been translating Spanish poetry and reading French surrealism, and the influence is clear in a poem like "In Captivity," whose relation to the literal is defiant:

Over the picnics
The dwarf star is eating the sun.
Each day it feasts on more light.
We were getting used to blank mirrors,
And snapshots of former aunts
Fossilizing in our hands.
But there's no closet like the night,

That urgent fur, and the stars
Afflicting themselves on the sky
As if at a nowhere wedding. Whenever
The lovers undress, they are
The white of calendars without days,
The white of trout multiplying,
And blank dice, thrown once,

And then never again.

Despite the macabre imagery and fatalistic, relentlessly negating rhetoric (for which Levis sustained a lifelong fondness), there is an intoxicated gusto to this procession of dazzle and a surrealist rejection of sense and poetic utility. The celebration here is of the imagination itself, with only an antithetical, sabotaging relation to the external world.

When metaphor is employed in its conservative function of equivalency, it acts as a device that focuses attention: "She was like a well-kept desk: her pencils were sharpened, her files were neatly stacked." In its more fantastical application, as in "In Captivity," metaphor acts as an end in itself—it is explosive, and it travels outward with barely a glance over its shoulder at its point of departure. In a poet like the mid-career Levis—what are we to call him? Visionary? Baroque? Romantic?—the escapist function of the image is always active. How a given writer employs metaphor is defined by temperament, and in Levis we find a deep abiding summons to dream, to enter a narcotic dimension of the imagination.

Though he did not reside for long in the radically surreal mode of "In Captivity," eruptions of imaginative energy occur through-out Levis's work; in part, they characterize it. As time went on, his images grew less aggressively sensational than those of "In Captivity," more intuitive and prolonged. His figurative dilations are more often leashed to discursion and narrative; leashed but not subordinated. Not technically or exclusively metaphorical, these departures are metaphor-like. In the reverie of a poem like "Lost Fan, Hotel Californian, Fresno, 1923" from the 1981 book *The Dollmaker's Ghost,* we see the same tranced, open-ended associa-tion as in radical metaphor. But in this later poem, the more ma-ture Levis makes a more prolonged, cohesive act of fantasy than in "In Captivity":

In Fresno it is 1923, and your shy father
Has picked up a Chinese fan abandoned
Among the corsages crushed into the dance floor.
On it, a man with scrolls is crossing a rope bridge
Over gradually whitening water.
If you look closely you can see brush strokes intended
To be trout.
You can see that the whole scene
Is centuries older
Than the hotel, or Fresno in the hard glare of morning.
And the girl
Who used this fan to cover her mouth
. . . .
Is gone on a train sliding along tracks that are
Pitted with rust.
. . . .

And as your father opens the fan now you can see
The rope bridge tremble and the lines of concentration
Come over the face of this thin scholar
Who makes the same journey alone each year
Into the high passes,
Who sleeps on the frozen ground, hearing the snow
Melt around him as he tries hard
Not to be involved with it, not to be
Awakened by a spring that was never meant
To include him—

The poem's gaze stays upon the Chinese scholar for another fifteen lines, then skids back to conclude with the girl who might have owned the fan. The fantasy is nominally enclosed in a quasi-autobiographical narrative ("Your shy father . . .") But clearly this poem exists for its sublime *distraction,* its almost decorative, incidental vision of a wandering Asian man of letters. For Levis, this trance state, this reverie, this expansive, temporally dilated moment at which Vision replaces Seeing, was the goal of writing. As his work articulates over and over again, that ecstatic moment is one of contact with something else, something larger, which by its nature defies description. Call it Essence, or Otherness, or Death.

Whatever that moment is, it is not about the closure provided by conventionally executed metaphor. Rather, it is the quest of the radical romantic for an encounter that either illuminates or incinerates the self. Image and metaphor were a way in which Levis attempted to encircle this presence.

That the mature Levis had arrived at an understanding of his own enterprise is visible in the assured, symphonic writing of his last two books. In the title poem of *The Widening Spell of the Leaves* (1991), we see metaphor employed to create an encounter that is both a departure and an arrival, both escapist and meticulously realistic. The poem recounts a trip through an Eastern European countryside.

I stopped the car. There was no wind now.
I expected that, & though I was sick & lost,
I wasn't afraid. I should have been afraid.

To this day I don't know why I wasn't.
I could hear time cease, the field quietly widen.
I could feel the spreading stillness of the place
Moving like something I'd witnessed as a child,
Like the ancient, armored leisure of some reptile
Gliding, gray-yellow, into the slightly tepid,
Unidentical gray-brown stillness of the water—
Something blank & unresponsive in its tough,
Pimpled skin—seen only a moment, then unseen
As it submerged to rest on mud, or glided just
Beneath the lustreless, calm yellow leaves
That clustered along a log, or floated there
In broken ringlets, held by a gray froth
On the opaque, unbroken surface of the pond,
Which reflected nothing, no one.

                          And then I remembered.

By the middle of this passage, the reader must forcibly remind himself that the speaker is not in a location in which any water is present. He is standing outside a car in a foreign country. One asks, *What* is this an image of? What is "the widening spell of the leaves?" Here we see an example of radical metaphor in which the local displaces the global, the shore is forgotten as the boat journeys outward. Reading the late Levis can be a disorienting experience because we are repeatedly drawn into another dimension, forgetting the place we started from.

Levis is not interested in metaphorical equivalence, in comparison as a device whose goal is logical coherence, or persuasion, or concentration; rather, his practice is to use image as a form of inquiry, as a kind of tentative, speculating finger poking into the unknown. That form of inquiry can sometimes sound very much like deductive thinking and sometimes like fantasy and sometimes like allegory and sometimes like hallucination. The heroism of Levis's work is that he seems (like his surrealist cousins) willing to follow it anywhere. As a lifelong student of Mystery, he was dedicated to his own ignorance.

When these two contemporary masters, Matthews and Levis, died some years ago, people said the usual things: they were too young, they were cut off in their prime. I felt the loss of two writers who had been my teachers for a long time—not in person but, for decades, in book after book. I also felt that each of these poets had accomplished a fullness of artistic expression, had reached a level in their craft that seems very rare in the half-finished world. Matthews's brilliant, mournful wit and his dogged, civilized arguments for contentment, and Levis's brooding, fabular odysseys are promontories in the landscape that survives them. Each writer played the hand of a given sensibility with brilliance, persistence, and courage, though the trail led sometimes beyond the hearing of any audience. The subject of this essay, their relationship with image, is just a small part of their legacy. Their poems, still in our possession, carry their images forward.

Obsession

("ARE YOU STILL WRITING ABOUT YOUR FATHER?")

A real diehard, indestructible, irresolvable obsession in a poet is nothing less than a blessing. The poet with an obsession never has to search for subject matter. It is always right there, welling up like an Artesian spring on a piece of property with bad drainage. It is a pressing subject that subjectively expresses; it will infiltrate the innocent description of a cloud and inveigle its way into the memory of a distant city. Emily Dickinson's critics say that death was her "flood subject," the theme that electrified her language whenever she approached it. A poet without a true obsession, a foundational fracture, a mythic wound, may have too much time to think. The poet without a compelling, half-conscious story of the world may not have a heat source catalytic enough to channel into the work of a lifetime.

The danger of obsession, of course, is the potential for redundancy: immobility, stagnation, narrowness of aperture, confinement, paralysis, arrested development. Neurotic recitation can be boring. The talent of Poet Z may be tethered to lascivious narratives of twenty-something erotic encounters—but can she write them for forty years? Won't the subject of choice eventually come to seem like watching colorized TV reruns? However, we should be cautious in judging the possessed writer. To say Poet Z is fixated makes it sound like a petulant and willful choice; better to say she is crucified. A well-known American fiction writer discovered his first full power in writing two novels about his Vietnam War experience. Despite earnest and ambitious attempts at a different subject matter, he has been unable to transplant that infusion of genius to another subject. His subject matter owns him. "And ghosts must do again / What gives them pain," says W. H. Auden.

Still, those without a primary force to drive and aid them, like a spirit guide, or a revenant, have reason to look with envy upon the blessed. Passion is the greatest gift a poet can have, and nobody is mildly obsessed. Violence of feeling can compensate for many other weaknesses in a writer. Stanley Kunitz advises young poets to polarize their contradictions, which we might translate to mean, "cultivate your obsession." Rather than therapeutically resolve it, try to make a full relationship with it.

In the work of a good poet, it is usually possible to discern one or two characteristic emotional zones in which he thrives: melancholy, rage, pity, vengeful rationality, seduction. A mature poet may not know how to command obsession, but understands how to transfuse material into it and then to surrender. The obsessed psyche knows unerringly where to go, like a Geiger counter to uranium, or a dog to his master's grave. Lucky dog, to have a master.

Sad Anthropologists

THE DIALECTICAL USE OF TONE

The purpose of poetry is to remind us
how difficult it is to remain just one person,
—CSZELAW MILOSZ ("ARS POETICA?")

A truly good poem seems, somehow, to breathe. It seems to hold not just interesting, valuable things in its interior, but also to install a kind of spaciousness around those things, and both space and matter seem to undulate in a flexible, rhythmic relatedness. The materials are not lumped or nailed together, nor driven down a corridor like a cow to slaughter, nor does the reader feel boxed in by the agenda of the poem. Instead, the poem seems an environment with stress and flex provided for. Much of this spaciousness and human flavor arises from the skillful employment of tone.

Tone is such an ambient, fluid, and internal quality in writing, one constructed from so many shifting elements (diction, music, pacing, image, syntax), that to define it is an elusive, probably impossible task. The baseline definition one encounters most often is that tone is 1) the attitude of the writer toward her subject or 2) of a speaker toward her audience. But even in such a general definition one sees omissions: What about the speaker's attitude toward the speaker? What about the speaker's attitude about her way of speaking?

This definitive vagueness about tone is understandable, and even necessary, in order to encompass the expressive possibilities of tone, which seem infinite. Perhaps the best way to say it is that tone shows the *how* of attachment: how the writer is connected to the words; how the words are connected to the world. Moreover, tone is the agent by which we sense the stakes of an engagement, and not just that, but also the complex system of detachments in a relationship. When a poem has good tone, we feel that it *breathes,* that the speaker has constructed a space for inhalation and exhalation. Tone is like that layer of air between your body and your clothes that keeps you warm and gives you room to move.

The best, most immediate way to illustrate what tone is, is to consider an example of *angular* tone. Tone is most visible when it is at an angle. Since the sense of angularity requires the juncture of two things, it is also useful to think of tone as a sort of fraction. Take, as an example, the opening of Wallace Stevens's poem "The Motive for Metaphor":

You like it under the trees in autumn,
Because everything is half dead.

These two lines introduce us not to a scene so much as to the angle of a sensibility. The angle struck here is the oddity of attraction to something that would typically be thought of as distasteful, the angle between attraction and repulsion, between the words "like" and "half dead." This fraction is the nucleus of the tone. How would we label this tone? Perhaps as mysterious, perhaps confident; menacing, macabre, somber, gleeful, defiant, sensuous? This tonal plot stands waiting to be built on, but it anchors the poem compellingly and firmly from the start. It initiates an emotional plot.

Here is another example of tonal overture from the prose writer Grace Paley, one of the most singular artists of American tone. This is the first sentence in her story "The Story Hearer":

I am trying to curb my cultivated individualism, which
seemed for years so sweet.

Before reading Paley, I would never have imagined that a story
could leap into being with this kind of instantaneous presence of
character. I thought such complexity had to be accumulated through
painstaking application of layer after layer. Casual, intimately direct yet terrifically sophisticated, the sentence makes obvious that to
begin from an advanced degree of self-consciousness is also to begin
at an advanced place in "plot." In this Paley sentence, we could say
there is a strong angle created between natural and imposed versions
of the speaker's self; between the earnestness of "I am trying" and the
socio-Marxist verbal formula of "cultivated individualism." The tonal
tension between them tells a history of the speaker's consciousness.
If a writer can, through tone, so vigorously jump start a character's
voice and narrative parameters, what might happen next?

When we emphasize angularity as the main constituent of tone,
this may seem identical to what is meant by irony; to be ironical, after
all, is to speak at an angle to content. Someone says, "Yeah, that was a
great vacation," implying the opposite: it was a terrible vacation. But
irony, with its implication of negation or undermining, is much too
broad a term to cover the subtle spectrums of angular tone, for every
inflection of diction and sound is not ironical in the sense of negating. When Stevens says he likes it under the trees where everything is
half dead, he doesn't mean that he *doesn't* like it there. In fact he does
like it, though he knows that this fact may make him a little peculiar.
Tone is not just the expression of feeling, it also includes the speaker's knowledge about feelings. As Ellen Bryant Voigt has said, tone is
a representation not just of the emotional immediacies, but also of
the forms of feeling.

Dialectical Tone: Louise Glück

On the most practical of levels, for both the writer and reader, tone
is often what announces and unlocks the plot of a poem, the way a
single crystal at the core of a snowflake determines the structure the
snowflake takes as it is built up. For example, consider the beginning
of "Purple Bathing Suit" by Louise Glück:

I like watching you garden
with your back to me in your purple bathing suit:
your back is my favorite part of you,
the part furthest away from your mouth.

You might give some thought to that mouth.
Also to the way you weed, breaking
the grass off at ground level
when you should pull it up by the roots.

How many times do I have to tell you
how the grass spreads, your little
pile notwithstanding, in a dark mass which
by smoothing over the surface you have finally
fully obscured? Watching you

stare into space in the tidy
rows of the vegetable garden, ostensibly
working hard while actually
doing the worst job possible, I think

you are a small irritating purple thing
and I would like to see you walk off the face of the earth
because you are all that's wrong with my life
and I need you and I claim you.

"Purple Bathing Suit" is a fine example of what might be called the
dialectical use of tone. The core narrative moment is simple enough:
a woman watching her lover weed the garden. It is not story, but the
layered, rhythmic management of inflection and emphasis that makes
"Purple Bathing Suit" such a forceful and rich poem. This is a poem in
which tone conducts plot. And because Glück is so skilled, we understand by the end of the first stanza the essential fraction of the tone,
the numerator and denominator: Attraction / Scorn; Attachment /
Resentment; I like watching / Your back.

Lines three, four, and five operate like a verbal nail gun, spitting
out the tonal signatures that anchor the poem, ensuring that we know

the speaker's feelings are complex, long-standing, and half-buried. By the end of that first stanza, though we are still information-poor, we are tone-rich, and we are deeply rooted in the emotional ground of the poem.

Those three lines also illustrate how tone evolves by building inflection upon inflection. Though we perceive that line three—"your back is my favorite part of you"—might be sarcastic, it still lies within the possible range of wit; the speaker might be affectionately kidding or maybe even making a sexual joke, i.e., "I like your butt." Line four, though—"the part furthest away from your mouth"—is so forceful that it shoves wittiness into the realm of sarcasm; we know hostility when we hear it. Line five withdraws a little and hovers offshore, with its more tentative, enigmatic suggestion: "You might give some thought to that mouth."

Versions of the dominant tonal fraction, Attachment / Resentment, are reiterated throughout the poem, especially and most explicitly in the last stanza. Although it is not necessary to analyze the entire poem, another moment is worth close attention, a moment that illustrates how complexly encoded, yet readable, tone can be. It is the sentence that begins:

How many times do I have to tell you
how the grass spreads, your little
pile notwithstanding, in a dark mass which
by smoothing over the surface you have finally
fully obscured?

Here again the dialectical elements are locked into a dynamically balanced sentence.

The tonally dominant thrust (Attachment / Resentment) of the sentence is presented in the first line. Immediately we recognize the phrase as the voice of the parent: watchful, critical, scornful, overseeing. In a flash, we understand that the speaker has spoken like this before, and this information suggests that she is something of a shrew, a hector. The phrase and its tone are familiar to all of us, and the power of that familiarity cannot be overestimated. It gives us great tonal security of location. This dominant thrust anchors us

Major tonal thrust:
Longstanding, hectoring, parental, punishing, pushing away

HOW MANY TIMES DO I HAVE TO TELL YOU?

your little pile notwithstanding

Reinforces major thrust
(condescending)

How the grass spreads
in a dark mass

and I need you and I claim you

Subtone: existential dread
and concerned warning (protective)

Counter tone (attachment, dependence)

securely to the poem and the plot—which we already were fairly sure of—and provides an anchor for the counterinflections in the sentence to come.

What is surprising is how the sentence develops: into a sort of warning about the almost supernatural, spreading, "dark mass" of grass. In that image (and the syntax that carries it), there are at least two suggestions encoded: firstly, a possibly protective concern for the husband; "we must be careful—the grass is spreading" the speaker says. And secondly, we glimpse that the speaker herself has a rather existential dread of this creeping, underworldly grass. This knowledge, of her grass phobia, allows us to recognize a hysterical, wounded element in the speaker's anger, and one possible source for her severity toward the partner. In other words, it inclines us to a potential sympathy with her. That's a lot of information.

And there is still more. In the middle of this odd, unwieldy sentence is a reiteration of the speaker's condescension toward her lover, indicated by the diminutive reference to his "little pile." Thus, in these few lines, a host of tonal fractions are enacted, containing both major and minor inflections. And the clarity of this emotional algebra prepares us for the fierce end of the poem, in which the speaker's vulnerability and anger are fully, explicitly named. It's worth noting how these tones are both multiple and distinct; nearly simultaneous, they are hidden inside each other, fused and amalgamated. Glück's poem masterfully employs what could be called the dialectical use of tone: a conversation of inflections installed around a singular moment.

Stable Tone: Jack Gilbert

Tone inside a poem is not always so overtly dialectical in spirit. Often tone simply supports content, or it remains fairly constant in the course of a poem—it establishes a certain tonal angle and then maintains that angle. As in this poem by Jack Gilbert:

Married

> I came back from the funeral and crawled
> around the apartment, crying hard,
> searching for my wife's hair.
> For two months got them from the drain,
> from the vacuum cleaner, under the refrigerator,
> and off the clothes in the closet.
> But after other Japanese women came,
> there was no way to be sure which were
> hers, and I stopped. A year later,
> repotting Michiko's avocado, I find
> a long black hair tangled in the dirt.

Here the poem's tone is stable. The speaker maintains a diction of factual, flat objectivity that is at a tonal angle to the intensely emotional story. Gilbert is practicing the poetic of show-don't-tell, ideas embodied by facts, but it's the angle between the verbal style and the subject matter that energizes the drama and forms the tone here: a sort of passionate stoicism.

But though the simple verbal style has an eloquent minimalism in relation to content, forming a sort of cool / hot fraction, it is stable. Even the grammar in the poem, we could say, has a stoical stability: four sentences, three lines each. Gilbert made one decision about his tone and then lived by it. His style, his grammar, and his voice all remain consistent. Tone actually is responsible for much of the poem's success, but other craft elements are more visible: image, story, and, of course, the title.

When tone is purely supportive of topic and remains at a constant level, as in "Marriage," it tends to be invisible, merged with the poem. When tone is swiftly changing and overtly dialectical, it calls attention to the speaker, and to the poem, as a construction.

Dialectical Tone: Jason Shinder

Jason Shinder's "Hospital" is another poem in which tone is employed as a dialectical device. Perhaps it is even more tonally active than the Glück poem. Like "Purple Bathing Suit," "Hospital" is a poem in which the tone dances around a singular narrative moment, pulling it apart, prodding it, and exposing it from one angle after another.

Hospital

While the machine is sucking the black suds

from my mother's blood and then sending it back
stinking clean into the pistol-tube nailed down

into her chest, I climb out of my shoes and slip

a cotton swab of water between her teeth;
her dentures sliding off the back porch

of her mouth. Nobody knows, nobody can ever know

how she has to pee, wrapped in a diaper.
But can't. The yellow eggs she ate one hour ago

already the shit in her bowels. And lonely.

head-hanging-from-the-balcony-of-her-body lonely,
darkest-passage-from-the-hairless-vagina lonely.

But brave. But lonely. Because I did not stay all night.

Because I won't. Because I'm going to pull out
her bone that hurts the most and break the back

of every word I ever said to her. The world is evil, mother,

And I am, too.

In its dialectical performance, Shinder's poem demonstrates what poetry can do better than any other literary form: take the distinct lyric moment and slice it open, expose the musculature and skeleton, label its most particular tissues. And the name of the instrument is tone.

Once again, the scene is simple—a man taking care of his dying mother. But the tonal plot is rich and complex. In "Hospital" the dominant tonal angle, the tonal fraction, is between the speaker's intense sympathy and his resentment.

To say that the Shinder poem turns on alternate tones of pity and resentment is true, but doesn't account for the rich variety of the tonal engagement. So many specific kinds of resentment are represented here: resentment of the heartless machinery of the "stinking clean" hospital; resentment of the mother's helplessness; disgust for the mortality and rot of the body, as represented in the harsh language *shit* and *bowels* and *diaper*; introjected resentment of the speaker for himself for his helplessness and detachment. Each moment has its angle, distance, and intensity.

Writers skilled in the deployment of tone are always, it seems, skilled ventriloquizers and quoters. They are good at "appropriating" voices and styles from other sources and employing them. In the Glück poem and again here, one can see that tonal variety is a form of pastiche, a fluent pasting together of attitudes and altitudes of diction and phrase. Tone, it seems, is a theatrical enterprise.

Again, let us examine the insides of a single phrase: Consider the tone of lines seven to nine, "Nobody knows, nobody can ever know // How she has to pee (. . .) / But can't." This is the mother's implied speech. Inside those empathetically ventriloquized lines at least three tonal suggestions can be heard. To begin with, the repetition emphasizes the mother's infantilization by weakness, which is suggested elsewhere (as in the detail of the diaper). But the repetition isn't just empathetic; it also critically suggests the tone of whining, childish self-pity in the mother's voice, as does her use of the word *pee*. There is pity here, but also an element of mimicry, inflected with a tone of the speaker's contempt. Placed in the position of compulsory witness (who clearly *does* know that she needs to pee) and inevitably inadequate caretaker, the son's resentment is implicit.

Finally, we can identify a more general cultural echo infiltrating the repeated phrase, "Nobody knows"—it echoes the refrain of the traditional Negro spiritual, *Nobody knows the trouble I've seen*. That, too, is a resonant echo that contextualizes the scene of the poem in a larger, far-reaching human commentary. What a mingling of tones is here: pity, contempt, horror, and lament.

The passage of *Nobody knows* is nothing if not plaintive, though plaintive clearly does not mean simple. In contrast, consider the strange, exciting elegance of the chant-like passage in lines eleven, twelve, and thirteen, about loneliness:

> And lonely,

> head-hanging-from-the-balcony-of-her-body lonely,
> darkest-passage-from-the-hairless-vagina lonely.

> But brave. But lonely.

These elaborate compound adjectives serve to suspend the drama of the poem, creating a kind of ritualistic interlude with remarkable tonal effect. They import into the narrative an innovative faux-ceremonial speech that transcends the immediate drama of son and mother locked in struggle. Though invented, these phrases invoke archaic formulas of both lament and praise. How does it work? In part because the compound adjective is so elaborate; simply the number of words it employs, the time given to it, implies the freedom of rhetoric from time. These lines seem to arrive from outside the frame of narrative time. The tone shift elevates us to a perspective from which we see the scenario of suffering and dying not as personal, but as a universal, perennial human passage, one to which we all will be subject.

Both imagery and grammar are operant here. In the first compound adjective phrase, "head-hanging-from-the-balcony-of-her-body lonely," the suffering body is turned into a sad building with a balcony from which the head looks down. The building is ornate, the suggested scene is of an Elizabethan stage play in which the head addresses the body beneath it—which could be a figure for rhetoric itself.

In the second of the compound-adjective nouns—"darkest-passage-from-the-hairless-vagina lonely"—the son implicitly sees and laments his own vast separation from the body of the mother, the isolation of being spilled into the world, and his naked, child-like mother's imminent exit from life into death. Here pity and praise seem to apply to both son and dying mother. The inventive dignity of the phrases suggests that these ordeals—the dying, the sorrow, the separation—are inevitable, and that there is something in them of the eternal, even of beauty. Thus such speech imparts the flavor of prayer and litany. Again, notice that the language seems distinctly theatrical and ventriloquial.

Nudging and stabbing, varying in intensity, loft, and emphasis, stressing this, then that aspect of the human situation, "Hospital" shows what dialectical tone can do with a dramatic situation. Because the tonal conversation has been so lucidly and variously conducted, we intuitively understand exactly what is happening in the surprising closure of the poem—that fierce surge of separation. Rather than be sucked down into the whirlpool of mortality, enmeshment, and help-lessness of the mother, the speaker chooses to align himself with the surviving, even if demonic, aspect of the world. (Coincidentally, this refutation enacts precisely the opposite movement from the Glück poem, whose speaker at the last moment dramatically acknowledges the bond between self and other.)

What tone does in the poem "Hospital" is create a complex architecture of relations circulating around the core of an experience. Tone makes it possible to focus and pace the drama, elevate it and demote it, pull back and then zoom in and intensify, change the angle again and again. It converses and it orchestrates.

Dialectical Tone as Combat: Attachment / Detachment

It may be clear from these examples that tonal dialectic is a sort of combat within the poem. If you look at the examples you will see that the combat is with a significant foe: attachment—with the loss of perspective that comes from the fusion to subject matter. Yes, that's right, being too close to subject matter can be a kind of codependency. Lack of space and relativity inside a poem creates claustrophobia and cliché. The employment of tonal variety is a kind of twelve-step program to remedy this sad condition. Tone fights for angle and distance. Distance is necessary for the exercise of tone—but not, it should be quickly added, too much distance. Detachment is not the goal of the dialectical poem, merely kinetic degrees of separation; dialectic is a fight for perspective, but not indifference or total separation.

Surrogate Tone

Shinder, Glück, and Gilbert write poems of the personal life, of psychic conflicts that build up pressure and cathartically resolve. Yet, as should be evident, the dialectical use of tone makes it possible to handle other occasions of ambivalence. In the tonal play of Frank O'Hara's small poem, "Les Étiquettes Jaunes," we see one way of handling an inherited poetic subject in a renovated way. The poem might be viewed as a response to the question, "How does a thoroughly modern, urbane poet write a poem in praise of nature?" The answer is that he must be both ironic and sincere, in tones alternately attached and detached:

> I picked up a leaf
> today from the sidewalk.
> This seems childish.
>
> Leaf! you are so big!
> How can you change your
> color, then just fall!
>
> As if there were no
> such thing as integrity!

So much modern poetry has been conceived in reaction to romanticism, as a way to avoid romanticism, but here we see a way to incorporate romanticism into a style without being suspected of it. Surrogate tone permits a kind of purloined romanticism. O'Hara's deliberately simplistic praise of nature may have its tongue in its cheek, but it is also, on some simple level, joyfully sincere.

Kenneth Koch is another genius of romantic-comic inflation and practices it much more systematically and heroically than even O'Hara. Here is section 9 of Koch's early poem "The Circus":

> The circus girls form a cortege, they stand in file in the yellow
>   and white sunlight.
> "What is death in the circus? That depends on if it is spring.
> Then, if elephants are there, *mon père,* we are not completely
>   lost.
> Oh the sweet strong odor of beasts which laughs at decay!
> Decay! decay! We are like the elements in a kaleidoscope
> But such passions we feel! bigger than beaches and
> Rustier than harpoons." After his speech the circus
>   practitioner sat down.

When Koch wrote this in the 1950s, he found a surrogate style for our collective loss of the rhetoric and sentiment of straightforward romanticism. Surrogate seems like a good enough word for what is happening here, and it is contemporary, too. In marriages where there is infertility, or other obstacles to procreation, the surrogate is the partner you employ in lieu of the reproductive partner you would *like* to have. A tone like the one used in "The Circus" comes somewhat between reader and writer, like a glove, but by ventriloquizing romantic grandeur, it allows the poet to inhabit the place of romanticism in a tone that is ultimately sincere. Thus, high feeling finds a body.

To repeat: tone is not just the expression of immediate feeling, but the expression of the speaker's *knowledge* about feelings, the speaker's knowledge about the *history* of feelings. Paul Goodman's well-known poem "The Lordly Hudson" is another example of the use of surrogate tone. In "The Lordly Hudson," the speaker is simultaneously mocking and affectionate, distant and close, attached to and detached from his subject, the beloved Hudson River and implicitly, New York City.

> "Driver, what stream is it?" I asked, well knowing
> it was our lordly Hudson hardly flowing,
> "It is our lordly Hudson hardly flowing,"
> he said, "under the green-grown cliffs."
>
> Be still, heart! no one needs your passionate
> suffrage to select this glory,
> this is our lordly Hudson hardly flowing
> under the green-grown cliffs.
>
> "Driver! has this a peer in Europe or the East?"
> "No no!" he said. Home! home!
> be quiet, heart! this is our lordly Hudson
> and has no peer in Europe or the East,
> . . . .
> Be quiet, heart! home! home!

The elevated rhetoric of this fanciful dialogue between the speaker and the cabbie is a way of facilitating the expression of strong feeling, even while protecting the poet from the accusation of unguarded sentiment. What is striking to note, again, is that the passion is ironized but not discredited; not only is the feeling not contradicted by the irony, it is in fact served up on the irony of the surrogate tone. "Be still, heart! no one needs your passionate / suffrage to select this glory" is such a magnificent reprimand to the inner romantic—fully cognizant that the era of heroic gushiness is past, it still manages to wear that romanticism like a cape.

Likewise, the literally decrepit condition of the Hudson, "hardly flowing," realistically acknowledged in the poem, is at an ironic angle to the praise being heaped upon it. What is really being praised here, quite sincerely, is the heart's affection for home. This is patriotism rescued for the twentieth century. And it is the skillful management of both attachment and detachment that makes it possible.

As Goodman's poem makes clear, poems don't necessarily need a lot of substance; it's not the *substance* that makes us want to read and read them again; it is the *management* of the substance that gives it intensity and dimension, which makes a space for our imagination and feeling to inhabit. In "The Lordly Hudson" tone is the vessel that holds our delight.

Deracination: Excessive Detachment

The O'Hara, Koch, and Goodman poems, to different degrees, contain friendly but ironic detachments as part of their tonal signature. What happens when detachment grows more complete, and attachment becomes less distinct? If too tonally disconnected from experience, a poem might become a freefloating artifact of style, or a manipulation of language as code, or a pitching machine of insider witticisms. Here is a poem by a young experimental poet, Peter Richards:

Which Oval Her Ministry

> Which oval her ministry sought to ignore
> depends on the crown she reneges
> back to when cushions (dimples despondent)
> suggest a rescinded corsage.
> She decrees three ovals crushed inside another
> might impact the flowers I shove
> out past the dune eluded for days, we constrict
> all the way blue into begun.
> All the way blue into begun, teach me the circles
> that erstwhile over the surf
> a light to confide in. Light from her scepter
> (some divers mistake it for depth)
> bores past the seafloor cataracting with ovals.

Readers of modern poetry will recognize this as an experiment in "pure" language—texturally intense, skilled in diction and sound, and substantially "resistant" in content in a manner that might be connected to Gertrude Stein, for one. This poem might conjure up critical jargon about indeterminacy and nonabsorbability, but we aren't truly inspired to do the labor of such engagement because the poem intentionally offers no clear axis that connects its language to feeling or experience. The problem here is excessive detachment. It is, to use a word I think of often as a reader, *deracinated;* it has no root system. Consequently, its tone is inaccessible, glib but unlocated. In its extreme self-consciousness, it is lost in the privacy of its own aesthetic salon. There is no useful tone here because there is no recognizable angle between means and ends. We receive it as a game, and it remains that.

From Dialectical to Dialogic Tone

As I think these poems illustrate, the dialectical use of tone is a powerful tool that can construct elegant, dramatically precise situations, both personal and public. And such poems seem to be the fulfillment of the Milosz epigraph with which this essay begins: "The purpose of poetry is to remind us / how difficult it is to remain just one person." Yet perhaps that is not the whole story.

For years, since I first read this couplet by Milosz, I have understood it as a concise advocacy for a version of poetry that I favor: a poem is a heroic act of integration that binds into rough harmony the chorus of forces within and outside the soul. A poem struggles to orchestrate, prioritize, cohere, and coordinate these potentially shattering forces. A strong poem represents identity without oversimplifying it, and the poem's internal workings are themselves an analogue of that integrative struggle. That is how tone functions in the dialectical poem. Dialectical tone doesn't necessarily aim at resolution, but it does intend to make a closely arbitrated relativity.

But it turns out that not all poetry is aimed at precision and hierarchies and the struggle of integration. Nor is all poetry anchored so specifically in the realm of the psychological. Dialectical tone can also be used to array parts and timbres of the world in a more casual kind of conversation. Which might bring us to the French poet Guillaume Apollinaire and the poetics he invented at the start of the last century of juxtaposition, collage, and surprise. Yet here, too, tone performs an essential function of dialogue and connection.

A good place to begin is to look first at an excerpt from Apollinaire's *Calligrammes:*

Ocean-Letter

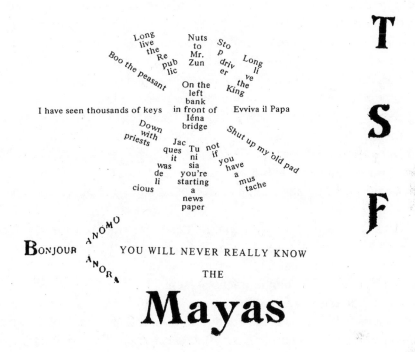

(Long live the Republic / Nuts to Mr. Zun / Stop driver / Long live the King / Evviva il Papa / Shut up my old pad / not if you have a mustache / Tunisia you're starting a newspaper / Jacques it was delicious / Down with priests / I have seen thousands of keys / Boo the peasant / YOU WILL NEVER REALLY KNOW / THE / Mayas)

This example from Apollinaire's 1917 collection *Calligrammes* is apt for a discussion on angularity, for "Ocean-Letter" is full of literal angles: it is a pastiche, a circus of fractions, dictions, scales, rhetorics, and moods. If you examine just one portion of this pseudo-postcard Apollinaire wrote for one of his friends in 1912 or 1913, you will see that the materials are vernacular, descriptive, political, random, elevated, pedestrian, multilingual, private, and public. "You will never really know the Mayas" he announces, and above that, in the little wheel, he adds, "not if you have a mustache."

The dialectical poems we've looked at so far practice a kind of triangulation on experience, aiming to capture the moment in a kind of pressurized dramatic container. They also are typically anchored in the psychological self of one speaker. In Apollinaire we find a non-adversarial poetics, a freedom of association with no distinct boundaries between the self and the world, or between one kind of speech and another. Put simply, he is not that concerned about closure. Such poetry is more interested in floatable relations than critical reconciliations, more in surprise and chance than the pressurized dramas of the self. More interested in happy disorientations of the self than its arduous unity. Here the voice is freed. "The purpose of poetry," Apollinaire might have said, in response to Milosz, "is to remind us how *unnecessary* is it to remain just one person"; or, how easy it is to be many people.

This is a poetry that feels qualitatively different from the dialectical. I would use the term *dialogic* to describe this mode, a term borrowed from Russian literary critic Mikhail Bakhtin. Like the dialectical poem, the dialogic poem presents multiple tones; but unlike the dialectical, such a poem aims to dislodge perspectives, not to achieve them. If dialectical poetry aims at integration, sanity, perspective, and conciliation, then dialogic poetry, like Apollinaire's, is about the experience of freedom and spaciousness. Here is what Bakhtin says about the dialogic power of the novel:

> at any given moment of its historical existence, language is
> heteroglot from top to bottom: it represents the co-existence
> of socio-ideological contradictions between the present and
> the past, between differing epochs of the past, between different socio-idealogical groups in the present, between tendencies, schools, circles and so forth, all given a bodily form.
> These "languages" of heteroglossia intersect each other in
> a variety of ways. . . . The novelist . . . welcomes the heteroglossia and language diversity of the literary and extraliterary
> language into his own work not only not weakening but actually intensifying them. . . . This constitutes the distinguishing
> feature of the novel as a genre.

Like other adepts of tonality, including novelists, Apollinaire is a skilled ventriloquizer of the human milieu. Apollinaire's representation of the environment of the self is as complex as anyone's. But it isn't pressurized in the same way as the dialectical poems we've seen; his poetic field is more dispersed and disjointed. Rather, a more musical, octave-shifting kind of collage is at work. Its poetic energy comes from surprise, contrast, and the rhythms of shifting.

Apollinaire's poetics are the foundation for much of the poetic technique practiced by the avant-garde and experimentalists today. But Apollinaire is readable and fresh still, engaging in a way that much experimental work fails to be. Why? Though he employs fragmentation and collage, his speaker is not alienated, nor is his relation to his audience alienating. He may be dislocated, but he is not detached. Even at his most fractured and chaotic, what anchors Apollinaire is his richly social temperament. In a poem like "Ocean-Letter," he is a magpie of life, but he chooses the vivacious and familiar tones of lived life: "Tunisia you're starting a newspaper / Jacques it was delicious."

Tone: The Brash Method

The practical question must arise for us as writers: How is tone learned and earned? And the answer must be, of course, that it is learned by listening, listening to the lives around us, both vernacular and formal, both internal and external, literary and anti-literary. But, like any writing skill, tone can only be learned by doing, by self-experimentation. In that sense, listening is not enough.

What the juxtaposition work of Apollinaire might make clear is that tonal vitality requires a willingness for violence and play. Bashing things together is one way to learn more about tone. And one useful poet, besides Apollinaire, might be Lewis Warsh, whose work practices a more contemporary manifestation of collage/juxtaposition.

Warsh, as a second-generation member of the New York School, has some kinship ties to the Apollinairian tradition of juxtaposition. The poems in his 2001 book, *The Origin of the World,* all follow a procedure of serial statement; some of the statements are narrative, some affective, some ideological. At times, a pattern that looks narrative, or lyric, or thematic, accrues some momentum, but it is quickly dislodged or undercut by the next unit of the poem. In other words, Warsh is a citizen of the postmodern, aiming at a kind of absurdist cognitive dissonance, an indeterminacy, an instability, a randomness. What such an elusive, teasing poetry does is expose to us our hunger for meaning, story, and closure. But if Warsh is hermeneutically punishing us, he is also engaging and entertaining us. Here are the first twenty lines of the poem, "More Than You Know":

More Than You Know

What I hold in my arms could slip away at any moment

She was wearing her heart on her sleeve, but I didn't notice it

Your symptoms will go away if you talk about what's bothering you

There's a relationship between monogamy & prostitution that's better left unsaid

People obsessed with sex aren't usually alcoholics

No actions are meaningful unless someone sees what you're doing

A turtle crawled across the highway & was hit by a car

It's still dark out when I drink my first cup of coffee

Occasionally my lover confuses me with her father

It was more than just the way the branches of the trees intertwined, but how a whole living being seemed to be rising from the ground

You can't have everything, or so they say, so I settled for a
cattle prod & a bowl of prunes

Proust used to stay in this hotel when he was in town

I finished the poem & put it in my drawer without showing it
to anyone

He bought a coffin for his wife while she was still alive

It might be possible to rent a BMW or a Volvo & drive
through town without killing anyone

There's pleasure in creating something, whether anyone sees
it or not

There are stalagmites, evoking pain, hanging from the wall of
the cave

I took her for granted & she left me for a man ten years
younger

A subtheme of this essay is the necessity for the poet to be both attached and detached from the poem, to be committed and not at all
committed to the content. "More Than You Know" is an interesting
case in point. Warsh's employments of angularity are appealing and
provocative, even if his ends seem vague. In an anarchic, nonadditive
poem like this, a critic might say the poet lacks sufficient interest in
precision, not to mention closure. Ultimately, these unmoored lines
are not sufficiently attached to acquire what is called poetic power.
Yet, in the classroom, I found that Warsh's poetic method animated
students with the freedom of insincerity. Freed from the burden of
truth-telling and fidelity, my students wrote their most tonally interesting lines and poems of the year. It was the disjunctiveness of
the poems that stimulated them, that issued them the invitation to
be enigmatic and unpleasant, to try on and discard tones in succes-
sion, to collage and juxtapose. When they put their sincerity aside

and their anxiety about making a poem follow through, they woke to inventive possibilities of the individual poetic instant. Freeing them from subject matter enabled them to remember writing as a playful and athletic enterprise, to teach themselves new gestures, gestures made purely of tone.

This incident was instructive; it offered a kind of proof about the value of the artificial, the value of the experimental, the value of inconsistency as a method, of thrashing around as a way of learning tone. Warsh's freedom from a set agenda, his lack of concern about closure or shape make a forum where a different kind of learning can happen.

Passionate Precision: Anne Carson

After presenting the Warsh poem as a way of suggesting the brash, vitalizing possibilities of tone-collage, I'd like to look at one last poet with a deep interest in the complexities of tone, though hers are more elegant, deliberate constructions than those of Warsh. In her book-length narrative sequence of poems, *The Beauty of the Husband,* Anne Carson characteristically employs a wild mix of both plain and highly wrought speech mannerisms. Here is the opening of Carson's poem XXI, extravagantly titled "Do You Ever Dream Poor Court-Bankrupt Outwitted and Lost of Terrible Little Holes All Over Everything What Do Those Dreams Mean?":

> Little holes that show where the rain hits.
> > He was not wrong that sad anthropologist who told us
> > the primary function of writing is to enslave human
> > > beings.

Carson's instincts are, in fact, not all that far off from collage, as is shown by the almost violent stylistic contrast between her titles and her text: one excessive and helpless, the other controlled and austere. In the second sentence itself, Carson shows how austerity and syntactical indirectness can channel great assertive force. The tone is one of reserve; the speaker's understatement is at an angle to the import of what is being said. Syntactically, the most charged information, "to enslave human beings" is held in reserve till the end of the

sentence. Similarly, the phrase, "He was not wrong," is a negative formulation known to rhetoricians as litotes, an indirect, patrician manner of backing into an assertion. It is not really a qualification—(the
anthropologist is indeed right), but it creates an effect of regretful-
ness, implying that one would prefer he had been wrong. A similar
tonal reserve is contained in the adjective-noun of "sad anthropologist," quietly suggesting a complex thing: that to possess knowledge is
to be possessed by sorrow.

But in order to truly appreciate the great indirectness and tonal
precision of this sentence, one must also know the context in which
it appears: its angular relation to the body of the narrative it is ap-
pended to. *The Beauty of the Husband* is not (as this sentence might
suggest) an essay, but a highly personal, autobiographical, almost confessional story of infidelity, betrayal, and heartbreak. In that narrative, the unfaithful husband's written and spoken promises have been
a persistent motif. The coolness and obliquity of the sentence grows
increasingly poignant only as the reader contemplates its relevance
to the narrative. One sees that the speaker is herself a sad anthropologist of her experience, and that she knows, from the antiquity of her
own sentience, about the enslaving power of language. Break it into
short lines, and the play between tonal integers becomes more vivid:

He was not wrong
that sad anthropologist
who told us
the primary function of writing
is to enslave
human beings.

We commonly think of tone as a kind of supplementary aid to our
writing and reading experience, a sort of vapor or undercurrent that
confirms and endorses what we already intuit. But Carson's poetry,
even in this short sample, makes clear that tone is extraordinarily vec-
tored in its own right. It is powerfully and precisely directive. It holds
many things simultaneously in its vision, and it positions them with inflection and counterpoint. The result is a rich and structured spaciousness that resembles, more than anything, sentience itself, rife with implicit histories of injury and hope, knowing and not knowing.

We used to talk about a writer finding his or her "voice," a term that now may seem outdated and naïve to some. But when I encounter a writer with a distinctive tone, like Carson, Paley, or Koch, I feel practically drunk for the way that voice draws into perspective big portions of the real that had previously seemed out of reach. That perspective is rich with attachments and detachments, a history of feelings and values. What we listen for in writing is a way of being in the world, a way of knowing. Skillful use of tone shows that the speaker cares, yes, but also shows how she is careful. How you hold it is what you know: that is tone.

On Disproportion

For the purpose of generalizing, the world of poems could be divided into two large camps: the classically wrought, well-behaved, shapely poem, and the deformed, lopsided, zany, and subversive poem. Of course, most poems don't exclusively belong to either category—they are neither Democrats or Republicans; they don't wear jerseys stenciled with A for Apollonian or D for Dionysian. Any good poem is an act of taming the savage or savaging the tame. Even the best-mannered poem holds certain opposing energies in dynamic balance and bulges with the effort. Likewise, poems admirable for their lack of orthodontia obviously possess qualities of integrity and unity, of proportion, that make them recognizable as poems.

Nevertheless, proportion is one of those defining aesthetic yard-sticks for a poet: the appetite for formal perfection is at odds with the appetite for losing control. This essay wishes to make the general case for conscious indulgence in stylistic effects and for indulgence of the unconscious impulses that occur in our writing—even when such indulgences distort the "packaging" of the poem.

Choices about whether to be formal or not are freighted with not just aesthetic but moral connotations. When we explore the literature of innovation and distortion, the relationship between the *formed* and the *deformed,* we discover that form and value are perennially associated. Such proscriptive tendencies are visible in Horace's advice in "The Art of Poetry":

> If a painter chose to set a human head on the neck and shoulders of a horse, to gather limbs from every animal and clothe them with feathers from every kind of bird, and make what at the top was a beautiful woman have ugly ending in a black fish's tail—when you were admitted to view his picture, would you refrain from laughing, my good friends? . . . . such a picture in which, like a sick man's dreams, the images shall be impossible, in the sense that no two parts correspond to any one whole. . . . this [imaginative] liberty [does not mean] that savage should mate with tame, that serpents should couple with birds, or lambs with tigers.

When Horace issues his manifesto of do's and don'ts, we observe that his allegiance belongs to a rather naturalistic poem, a somewhat realistic, mimetic poem. We also notice that his persuasive technique is social—he threatens us with ridicule. To the fantastic art he criticizes, he assigns perversity and unwholesomeness; it is "like a sick man's dreams." And what about the abundant, grotesque mythological imagery that furnishes his negative examples—mermaids, griffons, flying snakes? But Horace, Horace himself likes art that harmonizes and subordinates parts to a whole; art that keeps things or places things in perspective. Horace was an exceptionally sane poet. If we want to see his artistic ideals embodied, we might study one of his own poems, "Rectius Vives"—"Live with Rectitude":

> The proper course in life, Licinius,
> is neither always to dare the deep, nor,
> timidly chary of storms, to hug
> > the dangerous shore.
>
> Who values most the middle way
> avoids discreetly both the squalor

of the slum and a palace liable
    to excite envy.

The gale shakes most the lofty pine,
tall towers fall with the louder
crash and the highest peaks most often
    are struck by lightning.

Hopeful in evil times and cautious
in good, ready for weal or woe,
be prepared. Jupiter imposes
    the ugly winter,

but then withdraws it. Bad luck
is not for ever: Apollo varies
his archery sometimes by harping
    to waken the Muse.

In difficult straits show spirit
and fortitude, but on the other hand
always shorten sail when you
    run before the wind.

Really, it is remarkable, reading this essay-poem written twenty
centuries ago, to observe how persistent certain expectations about
poetry have been. The poetic standard of many contemporary poets
is very congruent with Horace's model. In means as well as theme,
"Rectius Vives" is classically proportioned. As it is a poem about
keeping one's wits amid changing circumstances, the concrete materials of the poem are constantly shepherded and overseen by their
own regularly reiterated thesis: "the middle way is best, be prepared."
In good essay form, the poem builds its case, sandwich-like, with alternate layers of assertion and illustration. The poem achieves its
"depth," its third dimension, as the reader's eye is directed back
and forth between the levels of the universal and particular. The
imagery—drawn principally from weather and navigation—is consistent in nature and degree, type and scale. These figures digress
but briefly and always relevantly. The poem never "adheres" to its

details or lingers over them, but proceeds at a steady pace. Formal yet fluent, rhetorical yet conversational, the style itself is a model of temperance.

Here is another, more contemporary example of the "well-proportioned poem," William Carlos Williams's "Pastoral:"

> The little sparrows
> hop ingenuously
> about the pavement
> quarreling
> with sharp voices
> over those things
> that interest them.
> But we who are wiser
> shut ourselves in
> on either hand
> and no one knows
> whether we think good
> or evil.
>   Meanwhile,
> the old man who goes about
> gathering dog-lime
> walks in the gutter
> without looking up
> and his tread
> is more majestic than
> that of the Episcopal minister
> approaching the pulpit
> of a Sunday.
>   These things
> astonish me beyond words.

The conventions of this poem seem all Williams, in numerous ways: in its descriptive method, in its celebration (and canonizing) of the unpoetic ordinaries of dog-lime and sparrow. The style has an appealing plainness and directness that seem open and American, a style that is itself exemplary of its message. For all its apparent spontaneity and openness, though, Williams's poem, like Horace's, is didactic in its intention and argumentative in structure. And, despite its spirit of democratic subversiveness, its poetic proportions could be called architectural and conservative. It is a formal, not a mimetic, concern for proportion that accords each character in the poem a roughly equal number of lines—two pairs of examples are comparatively described to illustrate the thesis—that birds are superior to people and dog-lime gatherers more noble than Episcopal ministers. The poem has economy and balance; numerically, the number of lines and words assigned each "frame" of the poem accords with the conceptual hierarchy endorsed by the poem: seven lines for sparrows; six for humans; dog-lime gatherers, six; ministers, three.

The three sections of the poem are basically equal in conceptual and linguistic weight; the poem maintains a consistent distance from its scenery and topic. It is symmetrical, clear. Though the suburban landscape, juxtaposed with the poem's title, declares that this is a re-visioning of the traditional pastoral, the title of the poem nonetheless declares its consciousness of its literary and formal heritage. Its paternity, like its formal balance, is clear.

This type of poem, I think—the poem-essay—mirrors many of the expectations we often bring to poems, whether we happen to be reading or writing them. We are *trained* to expect proportion in verbal art, and there are reasons we respond to it.

Oscar Wilde, in his essay "The Decay of Lying," has interesting things to say about proportion and about the source of our deep hunger for order and scale:

Enjoy nature! I am glad to say that I have entirely lost that faculty. . . . What art really reveals to us is nature's lack of design, her curious crudities, her extraordinary monotony, her absolutely unfinished condition. . . . If nature had been comfortable, mankind would never have invented architecture, and I prefer houses to the open air. In a house we all feel the proper proportions. Everything is subordinated to us. . . . Egotism itself, which is so necessary to a proper sense of human dignity, is entirely the result of indoor life.

Wilde's praise of housing, which is also his praise of art, implies that making art is a matter of editing and arranging. Though he concedes that such order may be illusory, he doesn't care. He is more frank than most artists about the ego drive that lurks behind making and the need to make the ego feel safe. The goal, as he presents it, is security; the method for achieving it is subordination: subordination, for example, of illustration to concept. Similarly, in a clean, well-lighted poem, we might suppose that the use of figurative language would be rationed carefully; likewise, extraneous details might be eliminated. Control, control! Psychologically speaking, the word *repression* might be appropriate here.

This may sound like a harsh summation of the proportion agenda, but most of us have internalized it anyway. We reveal the presence of such biases when we say a poem should be "economical" and "efficient," or when we apply commercial terminology to art: we go to *work*shop, not to playshop, where we decide whether a poem *earns* our attention or not. A real poem gets its *work* done without dallying or distraction. But, of course, control has a cost, too: it is often achieved at the expense of discovery and spontaneity.

What is art that does not subordinate parts to the whole, or to the self, or offer perspective? Such art might be called *insubordinate,* and it is a variety of insubordinations that I wish to turn to and admire.

Disproportion as Extravagance: Wallace Stevens

I think Wallace Stevens may have been the first poet whose work I recognized as deliberately excessive. Stevens is sometimes called *baroque,* a term once used to describe irregularly shaped pearls. Applied to literature, *baroque* is defined as "the breaking up and intermingling of classical forms" to achieve "elaborate, grandiose, energetic, and sometimes highly dramatic effects."

There are so many kinds of excess in Stevens to admire; or, depending on your temperament, to dislike. An inexperienced reader when I first came to him, deaf to most nuances of language, I think I needed a style as potent and clownish as his to alert me to the existence of such a thing as style and its possibilities. It might have been the spontaneity of the second of the first two stanzas of the poem "Loneliness in Jersey City" that first intrigued me:

> The deer and the dachshund are one.
> Well, the gods grow out of the weather.
> The people grow out of the weather;
> The gods grow out of the people.
> Encore, encore les dieux . . .
>
> The distance between the dark steeple
> And cobble ten thousand and three
> Is more than a seven-foot inchworm
> Could measure by moonlight in June.

What, I had to ask myself, was a stanza that seemed to belong to the oeuvre of Dr. Seuss (his *Circus McGurkus* period) doing in a poem by the renowned Wallace Stevens, a poet noted for his formidable difficulty and dignity? What was metaphysical assertion—"The gods grow out of the people"—doing framed by the Howdy-Doody rhythms of nursery rhyme? These incongruities attuned me thereafter to be on the lookout for other tonal exaggerations in Stevens's work and to interpret them as playfulness rather than loftiness. Thus while Stevens, in poems like "Sunday Morning" or "The Idea of Order at Key West," is admired for his grandeur, it was the grandiose Stevens that I loved; it was the mock-heroic rather than the heroic, the polka rather than the waltz, the tuba and pennywhistle rather than the violin sonata.

Perhaps here I learned something of the possible role of self-indulgence and spontaneity in writing; that pleasure was permissible as an end in itself; that insubordination was possible; that a poem could be elastic in form instead of architectural, more Slinky than Grecian urn.

Consider the shameless sonic extravagance of the beginning of "Bantams in Pine-Woods":

> Chieftain Iffucan of Azcan in caftan
> Of tan with henna hackles, halt!

Damned universal cock, as if the sun
Was blackamoor to bear your blazing tail.

Fat! Fat! Fat! Fat! I am the personal.
Your world is you. I am my world.

"I am my world," says Stevens, in these erratically linked, eruptive couplets. Is this the cry of a major poet, or a giant sophisticated infant? If maturity is defined as the ability to defer immediate gratification in favor of long-range goals—as surely patient Horace would contend—Stevens is an often immature poet.

But it is not so simple as that. Stevens leads us to appreciate that excess and pleasure are, if not synonymous, at least related. Freud calls pleasure as motivator the "pleasure principle" and saw it accurately as the adversary of hierarchical, organized, "adult" civilization. Adulthood, he says, requires not only restraint, but also the internalizing of social structures, hierarchies, priorities, taboos, deferments. And of course, much of our best poetry is exactly about such growing up, about the recognition of and necessary compromise with external realities. The architectural poetry of perspective, one might argue, undertakes the reorganization of desire in the context of possibility and limitation.

Yet Stevens never quite learned this lesson. Instead, it is exactly the independence of song from factual responsibility, the self-sufficiency of art, the joys of self-creation that compose easily half of Stevens's theme. His love of stylistic excess, his willingness to gallop off, to allow language to balloon into clause upon clause, is partly related to his nature as a lyric poet. He is innately more engaged with the passionate moment than with the long perspective. He celebrates experience, or he creates it, but he is not really interested in hierarchizing it. In many ways, Stevens's poems are *poorly* organized; or rather, they are organized by their self-generating music and whimsical associations rather than by beginnings, middles, and ends, by story or argument. There are no true narratives in Stevens, and few "facts"—typically, his images have an insubstantial quality, linguistic slide shows that bloom and vanish on the billowing clouds of his lyric.

This pleasure-oriented style, rather than any concept or event, is clearly the *originating* impulse for many of Stevens's poems. "The Bird with the Coppery Keen Claws," to take one example, is a fantasy about a supreme parakeet. Or consider the alchemical exaggerations of "Sea Surface Full of Clouds," all pomp and style if ever a poem was, with its oceanic, masturbatory, rhythmic description of the same scene over and over again with variations:

> The slopping of the sea grew still one night
> And in the morning summer hued the deck
>
> And made one think of rosy chocolate
> And gilt umbrellas.
> . . . .
> The slopping of the sea grew still one night.
> At breakfast jelly yellow streaked the deck
>
> And made one think of chop-house chocolate
> And sham umbrellas.
> . . . .
> The slopping of the sea grew still one night
> and a pale silver patterned on the deck
>
> and made one think of porcelain chocolate
> and pied umbrellas.

And so on. Stevens's excess here is brazenly loyal to pleasure rather than wisdom, to fantasy rather than fact, to excess rather than economy or utility. This stance against the reality principle is in part spiritual, asserting the transformative power of the imagination over the real. But it is also political, dynamically and intentionally pitted against the powerful superego of poetic tradition that designates the poet as merchant of meaning, custodian of morality, etc.

The pleasure principle in Stevens is the source of not just comic, mock-elegant effects, but of a great, sometimes far-reaching heartiness. It seems important to emphasize this point, the human value of flamboyance, in a time when the plain style predominates; when ornamentation is viewed suspiciously as "mere style."

Hyperbole

Stevens is often identified as a poet of high artifice and manners, in a tone that implies that the poet of experience is ultimately more valuable. And in fact, if style and experience compete in his work for the upper hand, style usually wins. "Sea Surface Full of Clouds" is not a poem in which the taste of experience dominates. But extravagance of style can also humanize: adding dimensions to a poem that a plainer, more conservative mode cannot.

One grammatically particular instance of such extravagance is hyperbole, that language event in which the naming of a thing inappropriately exceeds the size of the thing named. The self-conscious ploy of hyperbole is a deliberate lopsidedness, which creates an interesting warp in perspective. Stevens, (as "Sea Surface" shows) is a poet of special effects, and hyperbole is one of them.

The poem "Two Figures in Dense Violet Night" opens with a comic, bitter romantic complaint, staged through hyperbole:

> I had as lief be embraced by the porter at the hotel
> As to get no more from the moonlight
> Than your moist hand.
>
> Be the voice of night and Florida in my ear.
> Use dusky words and dusky images.
> Darken your speech.
>
> Speak, even, as if I did not hear you speaking,
> But spoke for you perfectly in my thoughts,
> Conceiving words,
>
> As the night conceives the sea-sounds in silence,
> And out of their droning sibilants makes
> A serenade.
>
> Say, puerile, that the buzzards crouch on the ridge-pole
> And sleep with one eye watching the stars fall
> Below Key West.

> Say that the palms are clear in a total blue,
> Are clear and are obscure; that it is night;
> That the moon shines.

There are multiple kinds of inflation here: the elaborately delayed syntax, the elevated archaic diction, and the complex figurative scenario. In the opening stanza especially, the speaker constructs a complex dramatic fantasy that counterposes an *I*, moonlight, the hotel porter, and the "moist hand" of a *you*. It is a comic scene, and in this elaborate burlesque of speech and imagination, we recognize a speaker simultaneously capable of insult, fantasy, and self-mockery.

> I had as lief be embraced by the porter at the hotel
> As to get no more from the moonlight
> Than your moist hand.

The particular hyperbole here is in the overstated comparison of the speaker's alternatives, in the fantastic preference to reality proposed— between embracing the porter at the hotel and holding his beloved's hand. This style could be said to be uneconomical—it is the marriage of a lot of verbiage to a little bit of situation—but the result of the inflation is that it immediately creates a margin of safety between spectator and situation and installs the reader in that safe spacious zone of speculative rhetoric, where he or she is free to admire and enjoy the speaker's ability to inflect reality. Both experience and style are in the room—but we know that the gap between words and things is large, and that we are floating in the roomy, spacious language half of the equation. The speaker's large personality is on display, more than a dramatic anxiety about outcomes.

From this highly stylized beginning, the poem develops surprisingly. Though the poem begins in linguistic vaudeville and anti-romantic mock-extravagance, it does not stay in comic register. It is as if that opening stanza establishes a high rhetorical plane that enables the poet to segue from a sort of boozy eloquence into an invocation—an invocation we end up taking seriously as it progresses. This transition from mock-heroic to heroic, from grandiloquent to grand, seems incongruous, yet it is effective. The example demonstrates an important truth: our tolerance for inconsistency, our ability to change direction in an artwork, is higher than commonly suspected. In a poetic zone in which exaggeration replaces gravity, human nature seems to be more flexible.

Another example of hyperbole and of how a seemingly uneconomical style adds dimension to a narrative can be found in "'This is Thursday. Your Exam Was Tuesday,'" an early poem by Denis Johnson. Like Stevens, Johnson creates an extravagant distance between language and actuality to fashion a complexly accented perspective. This passage comes from the middle of the poem, a monologue from a speaker (the "you" of the title) who has failed:

> And then—ascending
> over the roofs, the budded tips
> of trees, in the twilight, very whole
> and official,
> its black
> markings like a face
>
> that has loomed in every city
> I have known—it arrives,
> the gigantic yellow warrant
> for my arrest,
> one sixth the size
> of the world. I'm speaking
> of the moon.

In this excerpt, we can see the poetic role played not only by extravagance of syntax and imagery, but also by management of pace, a sort of temporal hyperbole. The most literal-minded of readers might say that the poet uses twelve lines to say nothing more than that "the moon came up." This extravagantly slow description, further slowed by line breaks, does suggest, in a mimetic way, the physically slow motion of the moonrise. In addition, the unlikely metaphor, "the gigantic yellow warrant / for my arrest, / one sixth the size of the world," is, in its hyperbolic warp, both comic and stylistically effective in communicating the speaker's exaggerated paranoia. Moreover, its absurdity, plus the controlled unfolding of the passage in which the metaphor precedes its own object, communicates the speaker's ironic awareness of his own mental imbalance. Here style, and a highly controlled poetical excessiveness, make possible psychological inflections beyond the reach of the plain style. The prolonged, imaginative mock-Gothic suspense of the arrest-warrant imagery heightens our involvement and pleasure in the poem, and the "bump" of the literal, when it finally arrives—the flatly spoken "I'm speaking of the moon"—both recalls us from our involvement with the speaker's fantastic subjectivity and condemns us to a less exotic confrontation with the circumstances of the speaker's reality. Along with the speaker, we discard our excessive emotional and poetical baggage and see what is before us. Here we have both high style and dirty substance, stylistic pleasure in contradiction with the genuine seriousness and real despair of the poem as a whole.

The Ecstatic

One important case of disorder, of disproportion or insubordination manifested in poems, is that of ecstatic poetry, where we find dramatic examples of sudden lateral movement, disorganized surges of language and psyche that might be edited out by the Horatian style of poet. Though Stevens's inflections are majestic and pleasurable and spontaneous in their way, they are so self-contained and autonomous that they are a little like power steering. Dionysian frenzy is beyond them. Stevens is not really interested in losing control; rather it is a sort of omnipotence he proves with his songs. Because he isn't really penetrated by anything external, he can only give birth to himself over and over again. Stevens, oddly enough, is sensuous, but bodiless. He proves consciousness.

But the god of ecstasy is Dionysius, the irrational, sensuous, blissed-out deity who at birth was torn apart and reborn; this rending itself is analogous to the rending apart of the rational and linear by intoxication. The poetry of rapture embraces categorical confusion; it desires disorganization; its essence is the overthrow of analysis and narrative; it desires to lose control and enter the vertical moment, to forsake balance and escape from time and the self.

Susan Mitchell's collection *Rapture,* surely one of the most exciting collections published in the 1990s, is full of tilted perspectives and beautifully written, unconventionally proportioned passages. One thing that unifies the collection is a fascination with loss of control, both perceptual and linguistic. In *Rapture,* one ongoing tension is that between the desire to be consumed by experience and the conservative indifference required by life in the material world. In a style alternately plain and plush, alternately swooning with verbal sensuality and withdrawing into arch skepticism, Mitchell places rapture in a very believable, contemporary context.

Though one theme of the collection is the poverty of words to register emotional complexity, the poems delve deep into language in a quest for the ultimate in articulation, pushing the speech envelope toward incoherence or glossolalia. In a passage from "Cities," we can see writing allowed to dilate elastically, far beyond the bounds most of us allow in our more missionary, perspective-ridden poems:

I want something else in my mouth

Bread and butter, coffee and cream, blink and stutter

In the city where I was born
but not so fast—

I want something other
the *cough* in *coffee* and the *cawf* in *cough*
the d*og* in *doggerel* and the *dawg* in *dog,* not *god*
but *gawd.* Forget *gaudy,* forget *gaudeamus igitur.* I want
the gutter in *guttural* and syllables like crates loaded
onto barges rusted, planks swollen, gangrenous, bitter
as iodine and its ignominies, the conglomerates stuffed
into my mouth before my tongue
was pulled out by the roots, I want my crooked teeth,
    language
before orthodontia, the sounds unbarred, the buck

and buckle and overlap,

In rock and roll music, feedback occurs when a guitarist moves his instrument too close to its amplifier—the result is an ugly, screeching, burning sound; of course the sound is also produced deliberately. Here in Mitchell's poem, we see what happens when speech becomes its own object, pushing against the perimeter between music and noise, between language and the pure sensuality of sound that would mean escape from consciousness and the self. Pushing, in a very basic sense, on the limits of form.

Such moments occur in everybody's writing, when language is energized, dilates, balloons, proliferates, and begins to write us. That experience is one of the rewards for the work of writing. Yet I am also certain that such Dionysian moments are commonly trimmed back, controlled, wrought into shape, perhaps eliminated entirely to conform to Apollonian standards of economy and proportion. We edit such insubordinate language events because they don't match the rest of the furniture in the house. Having an elephant in the living room is awkward; it makes ownership unclear.

A passage from "Legend with Sea Breeze," by Tess Gallagher, offers another example of lateral acceleration. Gallagher's poems characteristically flirt with instability, yet their disorder seems to map, with remarkable precision, the rich fission and fusion of psyche itself as it occurs—though the cost may be "neatness." It actually feels possible to see, at times, the moment when the poet is seized by the muse, what the medievals called the *furor poetica,* and is carried away. For me these runs of interfused metaphor / thought / perception, when they work, are thrilling, passages in which the rational pace of standard discourse is thrown aside in a gallop of irregularly unfolding, often fantastic figures for knowing and sensing. "Legend with Sea Breeze," a refusal-to-mourn poem, shows the ignition and blast off of such a moment:

Oh my black horse, what's

the hurry? Stop awhile. I want to carve
his initials into this living tree.
I'm not quite empty enough to believe he's gone,
and that's why the smell of the sea
refreshes these silent boughs, and why
some breath of him is added if I mar the ritual,
if I put utter blackness to use

so a tremor reaches him as hoofbeats, as
my climbing up onto his velvet shoulders
with only love, thunderous sea-starved love,
so in the little town where they lived
they won't exaggerate when they say
in their stone-colored voices

that a horse and a woman flew down
from the mountain, and their eyes looked out
the same, like the petals of black pansies
schoolchildren press into the hollow
at the base of their throats as a sign
of their secret, wordless invincibility.
Whatever you do, don't let them ring any bells.
I'm tired of schooling, of legends, of
those ancient sacrificial bodies dragged to death
by chariots. I just want to ride my black horse,
to see where he goes.

The lateral, whirling extension and complication of the figure here
into a narrative legend is not tidy nor architectural; it is sidereal, digressive, frenzied. There are accompanying confusions: Whose "velvet shoulders" for instance, is the speaker standing on? To what use
is "utter darkness" put? What is clear is that the writer has followed
the bursting of imagination into psyche and language into bravado, "I
just want to ride my black horse, / to see where he goes."

Is it any coincidence that this deforming, disproportionate burst
ends with the image of a woman joined to a horse, the very sort of
image that our civic, civilizing poet Horace warned us about? And is
it a coincidence also that Freud, in his essay about the pleasure principle, anatomizes the relative position of the ego and the id thus:

Thus, in its relation to the id, the ego is like a man on horse-
back who has to hold in check the superior strength of the
horse. . . . the analogy may be carried a little further. Often
a rider, if he is not to be parted from his horse, is obliged to
guide it wherever it wants to go. . . .

Disproportion's Conversation with Formality

I would like to look at one more poem, Susan Mitchell's "The Kiss" and to consider how the poem is a conversation, even a quarrel, with its own structure. Like jazz, it diverges, sometimes violently, from its melody, while the template, the ghost melody, unplayed, hangs in the background.

Perhaps the feedback metaphor is useful again here; in poetry, a writer might create feedback when he or she feels overcrowded by the genre, by the set expectations of the performance; and at that point, maybe, feels it is time to mess things up in an interesting way, to change chords.

Mitchell's "The Kiss" begins as a fairly recognizable romantic narrative, then begins to distort and modify itself in ways that seem analogous to the dirty noise of guitar feedback:

> He said I want to kiss you in a way
> no one has ever kissed you before, a kiss
> so special you will never forget and no one will ever
>
> we had moved into a room away
> from the others where coats were piled
> on a bed, and in the almost dark the kiss began
> to assume baroque proportions, expanding
> and contracting like a headache   pushing winglike
>
> from my feet. In adolescent fantasies I used to
> think of myself in the third
> person so that when I kissed for the first
> time in a film of my own making a voice
> kept saying Now he is kissing her, now she is
> unbuttoning her blouse, now his hand
>
> the voice just ahead of the picture or the sex
> lagging always behind as in a badly
> dubbed film the voice

trying clumsily to undress them, hiding
behind a screen or hovering above the bed dovelike
a Holy Spirit of invention presiding over each
nipple, enticing erect the body's
erectile tissue, enflaming their eyes

to see in the dark hiddenness
of wordless doing, to watch, to keep watching
the edge of, the verging precipice beyond which
language, thought's emissary huffing
and puffing, or beyond which language's undercover
agent and spy, thought.   Now thinking back to

that time, I am always just behind myself
like a shadow, I am muteness
about to blossom   into mystic vision   or with some word

stick a pin into, fasten like a butterfly
on black velvet, though it seems forever since I
kissed the back of my hand, pretending
my hand was my mouth, my mouth
the man's, in order to know what a kiss was, teeth
gently pulling at the skin on top
near the knuckles, the way a cat lifts
its kitten by the nape of the neck, dragging it
to a dark place under a house, or

licking the inside of my hand up the heart
line, down the life line   I don't

remember who left the room first, though
when someone told me he was
a famous director, I watched more intently
as he held out a canapé
to his wife.
            Sometimes in the years
that followed I thought of him, his ornate

description of the kiss, which with time became
more ornate, his tongue glossing

the whorls and bric-a-brac, the Adirondack
antlers on the grotesque banquettes, the kiss
coiling round itself like a snail

a small Gongoresque affair with all its
engines thrumming, that description the most
memorable thing about him whose face, if I ever
really looked at it, I have forgotten,
whose mouth, whose teeth, whose tongue
did not open anything in me
but directly

presented themselves as one takes a pear or apple
into one's hand and walks down the street
not thinking about the apple
or pear, but simply eating.

When we run into irregularities like the ones encountered in this poem, especially since they are disjunctive, we have to ask if they are intentional, or the result of incomplete writing. Though "The Kiss" could conceivably be read as a poorly written exploration of an individual's sensual history—and in part it *is* the biography of an individual's sensuality—it also seems to be a mock-history, a pseudo-flashback that screens its real act of bending and distorting the shape of the poem. It might be useful to think of it as a piece of somewhat postmodern music. The discontinuity early in the poem is quite digestible, but the poem continues to break down increasingly as it proceeds.

The end of stanza two is the first clue that things are not exactly on track, in the description of the headache, which seems to get away, derail, or deviate from accuracy: "pushing winglike // from my feet." What does that mean? But the poem quickly regains its predictability when it moves into the flashback, meditative third stanza—a maneuver we all recognize as a convention: "In adolescent fantasies I used to. . . ." Again, we are relieved.

But our confidence is only temporarily restored, and from this point on the real disproportionate oddness of the poem begins to assert itself; the long, inconsistent, sometimes broken and redundant digression about adolescent sexuality goes on and on. That digression exhibits a lot of eccentricities, including what might be called "incongruous specificity," as when the voice is described as the Holy Spirit, "enticing erect the body's / erectile tissue"—an oddly technical description inserted into a sensual context. These odd, looping motions of the text are inefficient and mutually interfering. Nor is reference always clear in this middle section of the poem; syntax wobbles and shifts, breaks down.

Like many readers, I come to poems with structural expectations, with a template in mind; likewise, I am both excited and frustrated by the deviation of "The Kiss" from familiar structural models. And the diction of judgment that comes to hand so naturally—"incongruous specificity," "deviation"—reveals the moral baggage that form carries with it.

These strange holes and digressive loops the poem offers serve at least one mimetic function; they mimic the perceptual process the poem describes. The real subject of the poem is not "The Kiss" but The Unkiss, the missing central experience, obscured by hyperactive self-consciousness, by digressive and descriptive flurry. By the end of the poem, we ourselves are perhaps flustered, disoriented, convinced that we have experienced a kiss even though we have been absent during the experience. In these ways, the disorganization of the poem is psychologically expressive, as is its deliberate ugliness and disorder. A marring on the part of a poet who otherwise seems quite capable of making seamless art. What function does it serve? That marring or muddle in part seems to be a rebellion against the pressures of formal convention, against the well-planned and executed poem. Psychoanalytically, mythologically, we might recall Horace's pejorative mythological images—this poem is a strange griffon of a beast; a woman's body joined to a fish's tail, a snake coupled with a bird. As the imaginary replaces the literal and physical, linguistic excess replaces the anatomical actuality. The tame and savage here are laughably or horribly joined.

Conclusion

Excesses, I've been trying to argue, are good. In various hands, they demonstrate freedom, they give pleasure, they celebrate artifice, they react against convention, and they illustrate the healthy, complex earthiness of the maker.

The question arises, in discussing a poem like "The Kiss," how much digression, wildness, lack of control, tumult of style and content can a poem contain? Until rapture ruptures? The easy answer, and the only true one, of course, is that it will take as much as it takes. The final standard is whatever works.

I have a friend who once edited a poetry magazine and returned manuscripts with a note saying, "a little more savoir faire, please." Arch and arrogant, I thought at the time. Now I can understand, I think, what he meant, and reading many poems I, too, often want to say, "a little more excess, style, violence, savoir flair, please." It was Rilke, our great model for the ecstatic poet, who asks in the Ninth Duino Elegy, "Are we, perhaps, here just for saying: House, / Bridge, Fountain, Gate, Jug, Olive tree, Window,— / possibly: Pillar, Tower?" These lines, suggesting a life's work in the plain style, imply that an artist would be well exercised if kept on a diet of all nouns.

But Rilke the poet, in the poem itself, hardly slows down at his own suggestion; he whirls, pirouettes, leaps, spins, commands, begs, refuses—and goes on to add, "but for saying, remember, / oh, for such saying as never the things themselves / hoped so intensely to be."

For it is the job of the poet to give pleasure, to amaze and exhort as well as to testify to the real; to demonstrate the capabilities of human genius and joy. Song is heroic. It has its place even at a funeral. How else will we remember that anything is possible?

Polka Dots, Stripes, and Plaids

DECORATIVE INSTINCTS AND
COMPOSITIONAL STRATEGIES IN POETRY

Several years ago, when I lived in Washington, D.C., where museums are plentiful and charge no admission, I was able to visit the National Gallery often. When you don't pay eight dollars at the door, you don't have to assume an all-you-can-eat mentality; you can drop into a museum for a thirty-minute visit. At the National Gallery I would always end up in the same place: a small side gallery on the east second floor—inhabited by two Rousseaus, some Modiglianis, and, most crucially, four or five paintings by Henri Matisse, which seemed bottomless in the amount of pleasure-gazing they could accommodate and reciprocate. Standing in front of those paintings, I felt that I was transfusing pleasure directly into my optic nerve. Matisse's late paintings are often domestic interiors, like these—casually drawn and even casually filled in. Their energy, which is weightless and playful, like morning sunlight, comes in part from their earthy, bright pigments; and also from the way they house three or four patterns inside the same frame; a rug, a polka-dotted tablecloth, flowers in a vase and flowers in the wallpaper, the checks on a woman's dress.

There is no suffering in Matisse's paintings and not much, if any, narrative; their realism is perfunctory. They are not paintings about the depth of the human condition, don't feature the annunciation of angels to Mary; they don't have the visceral chaotic passion of Jackson Pollock, or Mark Rothko's aura of spiritual migraine. They don't tax the viewer in any obvious way; they are, literally, floral: they have an unmistakable decorative intention. In a certain light, they seem as innocent and undemanding, as purely compositional as wallpaper.

And what are we to make of that? We dramatists of the realm of experience, we dedicated realists or surrealists who shape, explain, evoke, and elicit insight in the context of difficulty?

Pattern as a self-sufficient poetic virtue has lost prestige in the time of free verse. The odd sestina still turns like an old Ferris wheel over the amusement park of yesteryear, but in modern poetry irregular shapes hold more credibility than perfect patterning. Technical and symmetrical perfections of rhyme and meter, famously, can seem empty. Nonetheless, decorative elements, sometimes cast in markedly new, almost foreign forms, are emerging in new poetry. This essay would like to consider the satisfactions and strategic uses of *pattern* in poetry, and to explore how a compositional instinct, a sense of composition like the one Matisse employs so beautifully, can achieve some unlikely and worthwhile effects.

For a poetic corollary of such decorative aesthetics, we might well begin with an American master from the same era as Matisse, one who had a keen sense of verbal pattern, and who also took advantage of "flatness": Gertrude, Gertrude Stein. Here is one of her *Tender Buttons,* titled "A Box.":

> Out of kindness comes redness and out of rudeness comes
> rapid same question, out of an eye comes research, out of se-
> lection comes painful cattle. So then the order is that a white
> way of being round is something suggesting a pin and is it dis-
> appointing, it is not, it is so rudimentary to be analysed and
> see a fine substance strangely, it is so earnest to have a green
> point not to red but to point again.

Let me begin by going out on a limb and asserting that Stein's poem has nothing to do with boxes. "A Box." is not an exercise in realism.

Rather, it is a word-machine that utilizes familiarities of syntax and reference to make a pattern suggestive enough to hold our attention. Its appeal, oddly enough, is largely decorative—rhythmic and flat, repetitive, linked, relatively continuous. One reason Stein uses so many monosyllabic words might be their uniformity as repetitive units.

"I tried," says Stein, "to convey the idea of each part of a composition being as important as the whole. It was," she modestly continues, "the first time in any language that anyone had used that idea of composition in literature." What does Stein mean by "that idea of composition?" She means a giving up of the semantic imperative of language. She means using words like musical notes, or paint, as a plastic material in which relative weight is determined by sound and placement, not by meaning.

Question: What about self-expression? Answer: What is so interesting about a self? Stein, after all, wrote a book called *Everybody's Autobiography,* which tells you something of her estimation of individuality. Surely she was given to sly, hermetic games, but Stein is also a connoisseur of the subtleties of sameness, a maestro of the sensual playful pleasure of pattern and indefinite suggestion.

Speaking of a similar poem by Stein, the critic Marjorie Perloff calls it "a kind of geometric fantasy." Elsewhere, Perloff makes another observation so useful I want to adopt its terminology as the center of this discussion. Perloff says:

> this tension between reference and game, between a pointing system and a self-ordering system that we find in [Stein].

This passage comes from Perloff's book *The Poetics of Indeterminacy,* and it is a concise description of not just Stein's but much experimental poetry, in which these two ways of using poetic language are competing or cohabiting with each other—"in tension," as Perloff says. In "a pointing system," a *wall* is a flat vertical part of a house. In a "self-ordering" or "compositional" system, a *wall* is almost identical to a *shawl* or a *wail.* The difference in orientation is the difference between using language referentially or compositionally.

Perhaps this sounds theoretical, postmodern, and daunting. Yet this split between types of contemporary writing and writers is quite a real feature of the landscape. In contemporary American poetry right now, the split between referential and compositonal work sometimes seems a definitive polarity. On the one hand, some writers speak of experience and representation; honesty, necessity, thought, and feeling. On the other side, writers think in terms of *method* and *text*; speak of poetic "projects" and "discourses." These distinct idioms are in part the difference between those oriented to writing as a compositional game and those who write in a pointing system.

What are the defining characteristics of the compositional poem or poet? A list might include:

—A greater preoccupation with language pattern than with content
—A strong, assertive sense of the poem as "text" as opposed to signification
—A corollary sense of the *arbitrariness* or *interchangeability* of the referent: it might make little difference, for example, whether the poem said "trowel" instead of "towel" or "diverge" instead of "submerge."
—A predilection for repetition and variation (à la wallpaper); making rhythm more important than melody
—A poem made by compositional instinct also might not have an identifiable center or edges; therefore, it is hard to tell where the poem should end, or if it needs to end; likewise (as with wallpaper) it is hard to say where the beginning or "climax" is.
—"Necessity" isn't a priority, in either selection or shape.

Here is another sample of what might be called decorative or compositional work: the opening of John Ashbery's poem "The Dusk-Charged Air":

Far from the Rappahannock, the silent
Danube moves along toward the sea.
The brown and green Nile rolls slowly
Like the Niagara's welling descent.
Tractors stood on the green banks of the Loire

Near where it joined the Cher.
The St. Lawrence prods among black stones
And mud. But the Arno is all stones.
Wind ruffles the Hudson's
Surface. The Irawaddy is overflowing.
But the yellowish, gray Tiber
Is contained within steep banks. The Isar
Flows too fast to swim in, the Jordan's water
Courses over the flat land. The Allegheny and its boats
Were dark blue. The Moskowa is
Gray boats. The Amstel flows slowly.

Ashbery's poem is three or four pages long, but I confess that I
have never finished reading the entire thing. On one level, Ashbery's
poem is a parody of the Pastoral genre, which relishes descriptions
of nature. On the other hand, "The Dusk-Charged Air" is a kind of
joke about the emptiness of language. Ashbery's poem is a purely
compositional exercise: ornamental, flat, without a center of gravity; soothing and hypnotic, potentially endless, rather elegantly written, rearrangeable without damage. Though resourceful, it's merely
a hunk of text, ornamental, flat, without a center of gravity. It's the
Nature Channel in a nice room at the Holiday Inn. The most common criticisms of Ashbery are suggestive; in their very choice of
idiom they show both a comprehension and a misunderstanding of
the work. Some say, for instance, that the emperor has no clothing;
others that the clothing has no emperor. Perhaps both of those statements are false. But clothing is very much the point for Ashbery in
his compositional mode.

When the game-playing spirit is combined with a semblance of dramatic progression,—more of a story, for example,—true hybrid in-
vigoration can occur. In Kenneth Koch's well-known comic poem,
"You Were Wearing," we can see the compelling, sly effect of combin-
ing a "pointing system" "with a "self-ordering" system. Koch's poem
nominally narrates a generic story of courtship and romance. But as
one reads the poem, the compositional system—the repeated linkage

of proper names (mostly those of famous Americans) with domestic items—becomes apparent, and the "language game" of the poem, not the dramatic narrative, becomes the driving force:

> You were wearing your Edgar Allan Poe printed cotton blouse.
> In each divided up square of the blouse was a picture of Edgar
>   Allan Poe.
> Your hair was blonde and you were cute. You asked me, "Do
>   most boys
> think that most girls are bad?"
> I smelled the mould of your seaside resort hotel bedroom on
>   your hair held in place by a John Greenleaf Whittier clip.
> "No," I said, "it's girls who think boys are bad." Then we read
>   *Snowbound* together
> And ran around in an attic, so that a little of the blue enamel
>   was scraped off my George Washington, Father of His
>   Country, shoes.
>
> Mother was walking in the living room, her Strauss Waltzes
>   comb in her hair.
> We waited for a time and then joined her, only to be served
>   tea in cups painted with pictures of Herman Melville.
> As well as with illustrations from his book *Moby Dick* and
>   from his novella, *Benito Cereno.*
> Father came in wearing his Dick Tracy necktie: "How about a
>   drink, everyone?"
> I said, "Let's go outside a while." Then we went onto the porch
>   and sat on the Abraham Lincoln swing.
> You sat on the eyes, mouth, and beard part, and I sat on the knees.
> In the yard across the street we saw a snowman holding a
>   garbage can lid smashed into a likeness of the mad English
>   king, George the Third.

The conclusion of the narrative in "You Were Wearing" is almost beside the point; the reader instead has become committed to the entertaining game of name-dropping. The complete accessibility of

Koch's poem, written fifty years ago and much anthologized, makes the point that compositional strategies are not intrinsically difficult, hermetic, or even intellectual. As everyone knows, children love all manner of verbal patterns of nonsense systems; so do grown-ups.

We can bring to mind many writers who have a decorative, compositional streak in their work. Think of Gerard Manley Hopkins, in whom the intensity of compositional pattern is always about to swallow the discriminating intelligence. Or think of Cormac McCarthy's western novels, in which passages of baroque, seemingly interchangeable lyric descriptions of weather alternate with passages of tersely told narrative, as if he wrote one with the left hand and the other with his right. Or consider the paradox of Samuel Beckett. What are we to make of him, whose texts are compositional in many ways: repetitious, monosyllabic, largely plotless, very flat on the page. You could take a sentence or two from one page in *The Unnameable* and transpose it elsewhere with no one the wiser. Yet saying that Beckett is wallpaper would be problematic.

Lynn Hejinian's poem, "Nights," offers another type of compositional poetics, in the manner of collage: still strongly patterned, it is a scrapbook of compositional and referential gestures.

Ooooh, oooooh, ooooh, says the voice of a girl:

I've been attacked by owls,
by owls with towels,
I've been attacked
by snakes with rakes.

    It is just this kind of ridiculous language, banal but lacking even banality's pretense at relevance and sense, that I hear in my sleep; I wake, feeling irritable and depressed.
    *

The sadness! the injustice!
It's true I want to know, I want to look
But what is it?
    *

The fingers leave their owls in a calm
Sleep figures the features

Sleep speaks for the bird, the animal
For the round and the residual
. . . .
The 23rd night was very dark.
it was cold.
My eyes were drawn to the window.

I thought I saw a turtledove nesting on a waffle
Then I saw it was a rat doing something awful
But anarchy doesn't bother me now any more than it used to

I thought I saw a woman writing verses on a bottle
Then I saw it was a foot stepping on the throttle
But naturally freedom can be understood in many different ways

I thought I saw a fireman hosing down some straw
Then I saw it was a horse grazing in a draw
But it's always the case that in their struggle to survive,
      animate objects must be aided

I thought I saw a rhubarb pie sitting on the stove
Then I saw it was the tide receding from a cove
But although I have strong emotions when I watch a movie,
      jealousy is never one of them.

One of Hejinian's main influences is Gertrude Stein, and the influence is visible in this quirky piece, selected by Robert Hass for the anthology *The Best American Poetry 2001*. Hejinian's piece exhibits both the strengths and the limitations of contemporary experimental writing and the compositional spirit. What appeals here, in addition to the pleasure of sound-play, is the rhythm of two different kinds of language juxtaposed, and the way this is done in swatches, like fabric samples: the snatches of goofy nursery rhyme, in a strongly repeated syntax, braced against sentences of casual but adult ideological statement: "I thought I saw a turtledove nesting on a waffle / Then I saw it was a rat doing something awful / But anarchy doesn't bother me now any more than it used to." It's the pleasure of stripes and polka dots: as readers we get to enjoy the absurdity of the juxtaposition and also to enjoy the oblique, irregular ways in which the two discourses interact—in particular how the adult voice might be commenting on the aesthetic principles of the text. Here in Hejinian's poem—in contrast to the earlier example by Ashbery—the reader is allowed the orienting contrast between foreground and background (child / adult), though the contrast isn't organized in a conventional way. I don't want to minutely explicate this poem, but merely point out how a compositional sensibility can fashion something strangely delightful, in part because of its lack of primary preoccupation with referential purpose.

Again, limitations of the method are substantial: the shapelessness of the overall poem, the lack of clear intent. Moreover, this poem would baffle anyone not already well versed and sophisticated in contemporary poetics. Despite its appealing playfulness and charming lack of pretentiousness, it really remains an insider art, decodable to very few people.

Another important American quasi-compositional poet, one who, like Hejinian, is often connected to the L=A=N=G=U=A=G=E poets, is Michael Palmer. If Hejinian uses compositional strategies in collage with the voice of a more "normal" speaker, Palmer joins compositional poetics to a philosophical temperament. In the ironically titled "Autobiography 2 (hellogoodby)," reference is disjointed, narrative is insistently undermined, and semantic accumulation is steadily subverted. A deliberate flatness is part of Palmer's aesthetic, his way of preventing language from serving as a pointing system. Instead, his poems emphasize their textual status and insist that signs are only signs. Yet Palmer invigorates this flatness in two ways: first, with a strong compositional instinct, and second, by developing an internal jargon of referential mythic glimmers. For all of its deliberate distancing from content, the poem manages to suggest the presence of an almost secret but urgent background theme:

Autobiography 2 (hellogoodby)

The Book of Company which
I put down and can't pick up

The Trans-Siberian disappearing,
the Blue Train and the Shadow Train

Her body with ridges like my skull
Two children are running through the Lion Cemetery

Five travelers are crossing the Lion Bridge
A philosopher in a doorway insists

that there are no images
He whispers instead: Possible Worlds

The Mind-Body Problem
The Tale of the Color Harpsichord

Skeleton of the Worlds's Oldest Horse
The ring of O dwindles

sizzling round the hole until gone
False spring is laughing at the snow

and just beyond each window
immense pines weighted with snow

A philosopher spread-eagled in the snow
holds out his Third Meditation

like a necrotic star. He whispers:
archery is everywhere in decline,

photography the first perversion of our time
Reach to the milky bottom of this pond

to know the feel of bone,
a knuckle from your grandfather's thumb,

the maternal clavicle, the familiar
arch of a brother's brow

He was your twin, no doubt
forger of the unicursal maze

My dearest Tania, When I get a good position in the courtyard
I study their faces through the haze

Dear Tania, Don't be annoyed
please, at these digressions

They are soldering the generals
back onto their pedestals

Palmer's grave, hermetic poem presents a challenging degree
of dispersion—its narrative and referential elements are deliberately incomplete and inconsistent. In compensation, its compositional rhythms grant the reader a place to stand—for instance, the
use of prepositional phrases that include proper nouns (The Book
of Company, The Tale of the Color Harpsichord, the forger of the
unicursal maze) is one repetitive pattern here. Likewise, the reap-
pearance of some "plot" elements, like the image of the philosopher,
provides some illusion of coherence.

Like the Matisse paintings with which this discussion began, strong
pattern and consistent tone keep the poem from seeming chaotic or
crowded. What makes Palmer's poem possible and effective, ironically,
is its textual flatness. In the first three couplets we are quickly alerted
and attuned to the patterned, even decorative, nature of the poem. At
that point, we relax, thinking "Oh, it's a sort of rococo." Once we recognize the compositional stability of the poem, we can enjoy what Perloff
calls "the tension between compositional and referential elements."
It is the deliberate disengagement from one-to-one signification that
makes both the writing and reading of the poem possible.

In Palmer's work, subject matter typically remains vague or un-focused, unnamed, yet seems to hover behind the compositional tap-estry of the writing. Palmer sets up patterns in imagery and discourse and then abandons them, but they are enough to hold the eye and mind of the reader. Palmer also wisely makes tonal and narrative con-cessions to his audience at various points in the poem—in the clos-ing couplets, for instance, that become a direct address to "Tania." He even acknowledges the "digressions" of his method. The weave of the poem is precarious, yet the composition holds, and the sublimi-nal themes accrue.

What are the themes of "Autobiography 2"? Disillusionment. The hopeless distances between everything. The disconnectedness of mind and body, thought and feeling, words and things, systems of thought and actuality. Things Fallen Apart. In its way Palmer's poem is darker and more direct than most of Stein, and Palmer is one of the few poets in the contemporary compositional mode who achieves real poetic power because of that urgent thematic undertow.

One might speculate that this poem could not have been writ-ten before our time, not until referentiality had been undermined so thoroughly and consensually that its disengagement could become a grammar of its own. Palmer writes in the doubt-saturated, ground-less zero gravity of the time after Wittgenstein; yet, like an astronaut dancing in the vacuum of a high orbit, he has learned to manipulate words into a new kind of poetic speech.

Interesting analogues can be drawn between compositional poetics and other art forms. Techno music is one in which melody is displaced by periodic, evolving patterns of rhythm that ask a differ-ent kind of attention from its audience. Then there is the odd parallel of contemporary poetry to painting; the belief of some modern crit-ics that "progress" in twentieth-century painting is marked by an in-crease in flatness—that, as Robert Herbert says, "modernism means the progressive renunciation of depth and three-dimensionality in favor of flat surface." Such deliberate flattening is visible in a sec-tion from a Charles Bernstein poem, in which the engine of the "self-ordering" system impishly emphasizes its flatness:

Not that I mean to startle just
unsettle. The settlers pitched their tents

into foreign ground. All ground is
foreign ground when you get to know
it as well as I do. well I wouldn't agree.
no agreement like egregious
refusal to hypostatize a suspension.
suspension bridges like so many
the hot Carolina sun. no, son, it
drummers at bat, swatting flies in
had to be proud not what's worth taking
pride in.

In Bernstein's piece the compositional system deflates our desire
to infer three-dimensionality or theme. It provides opportunity for
cleverness and the amusement of broken expectation, but little possibility for beauty or poetic power. Such aesthetic problems adhere to
compositional poetics. If every poem is a collage of textural gestures,
how are such poems unified? More important, how are such poems
memorably distinct from one another if they have no individual identity, no "organic unity," no one speaker, no one subject? We remember poems that have strong narrative or thematic elements, the rest
blur into each other. This indistinguishability of one poem from another, pronounced in much experimental writing, has to do with its
claim, or lack of claim, on experience.

Yet the era of purist poetic theoreticians has clearly passed, and
even mainstream poets, including several recent U.S. poet laureates, have been visibly affected by the kinds of formal playfulness
imported by compositional poetics. In much contemporary poetry,
pattern, not content, is the dominant vehicle of pleasure. In other
poetry, several verbal planes are being collaged together by compositonal systems. Such poems are neither entirely representational nor
entirely compositional. Out of hybrid combinations of conventions,
some poets are forging new styles. Their audience may be limited
now to the initiated, but their vigor is real and may be infectious.

How can the compositional impulse pragmatically supplement or
enrich a referential one in the making of a poem? Consider Harryette
Mullen's poem "Denigration," which combines a compositional system with a discursive mosaic of social commentary. Mullen's atten-
tiveness is bifocal, trained to both word-game and to experience. The

effect is a postmodern political poem, one which joins a decorative pattern to a relentless pushing of content:

> Did we surprise our teachers who had niggling doubts about the picayune brains of small black children who reminded them of clean pickaninnies on a box of laundry soap? How muddy is the Mississippi compared to the third-longest river of the darkest continent? In the land of the Ibo, the Hausa, and the Yoruba, what is the price per barrel of nigrescence? Though slaves, who were wealth, survived on niggardly provisions, should inheritors of wealth fault the poor enigma for lacking a dictionary? Does the mayor demand a recount of every bullet or does city hall simply neglect the black alderman's district? If I disagree with your beliefs, do you chalk it up to my negligible powers of discrimination, supposing I'm just trifling and not worth considering? Does my niggling concern with trivial matters negate my ability to negotiate in good faith? Though Maroons, who were unruly Africans, not loose horses or lazy sailors, were called renegades in Spanish, will I turn any blacker if I renege on this deal?

In "Denigration" we encounter the pleasure of verbal game in tension with the grave unpleasantness of its topic: American racism. Mullen implements her compositional pattern at the level of the syllable and consonant, by repeating multiple variants of the core syllables, "neg" and "nig," with their dark, emotional-historical connotative ties. Thus the poem is haunted and taunted by the echoes of "negate" and "negro," "denigrate" and "nigger." On the discursive plane, the poem poses as a kind of faux high school examination in which the speaker poses a series of loosely linked test questions about discrimination. But the discursive questions themselves are discontinuous, errant, and riddling (the third-longest river in Africa is the Niger; *bullet* rhymes with *ballot*). Thus the poem is both a vocabulary exam, a nursery rhyme, and a history lesson.

The effect of joining "dark" content with a whimsical compositional technique is unsettling and slightly disorienting. The compositional system serves to stabilize the poem on the basis of sound repetition;

but the word-game also distracts the reader's attention from the discursive aspect of the poem. In the introduction to *Postmodern American Poetry: A Norton Anthology,* editor Paul Hoover says that postmodern poetry "follows a constructionist rather than an expressionist theory of composition," in which "Method and intuition replace intention." Mullen's "Denigration" is indeed "constructed" and "methodical," but it also has plenty of intention.

Mullen's own position as a poet has an eloquent parallel to her poetics. We could say that as an African American poet she is subject to certain referential expectations: she is expected to write about race. But Mullen is also an ardent experimentalist. The title of her book, *Sleeping with the Dictionary,* indicates a dual allegiance to linguistics and experience. And, like some other black poets of her generation, she seems in many ways unfettered from a reductive obligation to write the "identity poem," to write poems centered solely or exclusively in racial identity.

"Denigration" might be a poem that has not been written before. The compositional system evokes and unsettles issues of representation and insinuates dimensions of power relations between reader and writer that are complex and penetrating, in part because they are subliminal, unresolved, unfinished. We can imagine how comparatively blunt the execution of the poem might have been without the compositional element energizing it, without this secondary plot about the changing distance between words and meanings, signifiers and things. Here, allegiance to clarity, exactness, concreteness— values we conventionally emphasize—might have been insufficient to make a strong poem.

In the after-history of rhyme and meter, it might be assumed, or claimed that compositional poetry merely recasts the deep human desire for recurrence and pattern. Surely there's some truth in that idea. However, compositional poetry, as the preceding examples demonstrate, is intrinsically more unstable than the canonical poetry that precedes it; it employs and explores the same pleasures, perhaps, but in jazzier ways, in relation to meaning. In compositional poetry, as in most postmodern poetry, the dance between meaning and non-meaning receives heightened emphasis.

The curious writer will not dismiss these developments out-of-hand.

To attend to them is not an ethical concession to aesthetic fashion. Rather, we "centrist" writers might be wise to recognize the continuity of such technical shifts with our own internalized traditions. A shift in focus, from one plane of vision to another, even from one terminology to another, has been known to liberate a poem or a poet at a crucial moment. In our skepticism, we might remember Matisse and Stein, two geniuses who engaged themselves in making pretty patterned pictures, then found the reason afterwards.

Fragment, Juxtaposition, and Completeness

SOME NOTES AND PREFERENCES

When Guillaume Apollinaire impulsively removed all the punctuation from the pre-publication galleys of his first book, *Alcools* (1913), he broke down the compartments of grammar in ways that would affect the poetry of the century that followed. A few years later in his *Calligramme* poems, when he positioned poetic fragments in spatial patterns on the page, he proved that white space and irregularity could be part of a poem's structural composition. The various poetics that grew from these technical innovations have been described by many terms: as modernist, as the "poetics of surprise," as "open-field" poetry, poetic montage, as "indeterminate," as "reader-centered." The poetics of juxtaposition, fragment, and collage have been practiced throughout the twentieth century, sometimes centrally, sometime peripherally. Many would say collage is the central artistic device of modernism and its foremost contribution to twentieth-century art. And in our own time, the mode—fragment and collage—is experiencing a conspicuous renaissance.

In his important, informative, and readable book on the origins

of modern abstract art, *The Banquet Years,* the critic Roger Shattuck
tracks the genealogy of early modernism in France, including the poetics of juxtaposition. Shattuck offers an assortment of the rationales
for juxtaposition:

> The Egyptians were the first men to dress stone so clean it
> fitted together without crack or fault. The past hundred years
> have attained a contrasting and less imposing goal—an art
> composed in the rough on the principle of interval and ten-
> sion between parts. . . .
>
> Around the turn of the century, the arts begin to resist the
> convention of arranging their findings in established patterns
> of consistency. . . .
>
> Juxtaposition, with its surprises and intimacy of form,
> brings the spectator closer than ever before to the abruptness
> of creative process. . . .
>
> The dominant trait of the prewar poems of Reverdy and
> Salmon and Apollinaire has been described as "negligence."
> To finish in the sense of removing all traces of sketch and
> struggle and uncertainty became the surest way of destroying
> the authenticity of their work. . . .
>
> Mosaic style, truncated syntax, cancellation of punctua-
> tion—all these devices increase the inclusiveness of his poetry
> by keeping it open to all combinations and interpretations. . . .
> the primary quality . . . is ambiguity. . . .
>
> The fragments of a poem are deliberately kept in
> random order to be reassembled in a single instant of
> consciousness. . . .
>
> Without causal progression, everything is middle. . . .
>
> The juxtaposition of heterogeneous elements, the art
> of violent dislocation, affects us slightly differently. We are
> thrown back upon a desperate effort of assimilation. . . .

Collage is really the practice of a theory of knowledge: antirational
and semi-intentional, it takes coincidence and chance materials as
part of its method and inspiration. By eliminating transition, it em-

braces ambiguity, improvisation, speed, and multiplicity of meaning. It is expressive, but not primarily self-expressive. It does not place priority on closure, nor on conventional notions of completeness. In the constant conversation between unity and disunity, juxtaposition plays with omission and collision. It loves the energy of disruption and dislocation. Apollinaire, his contemporaries, and their aesthetic heirs were more interested in creating inventive disorientations than in delivering packaged unities.

For the sake of fixing a usable terminology, one way to put it might be this: fragment is the unit, juxtaposition is the method, collage is the result. When you juxtapose two fragments next to each other, without transition, you get collage. In fact, when you place any two dissimilar units side by side—even complete sentences, even paragraphs—they acquire the quality of fragment because they are not completed by their surroundings. The fractured poem may be relatively linear and continuous, or it may be radically disjunctive, but when transition is removed, relations become implicit, not explicit. Content may be whole or partial, or it might even be deliberately absent, to be provided by the reader.

What we get, at one end of the spectrum, is something like "Festival," one of Apollinaire's strangely buoyant wartime poems. In "Festival," the spectacle of flares above the WWI battlefield (where Apollinaire was in the artillery) provokes an associative soliloquy from the speaker:

> Fireworks in steel
> How delightful is this lighting
>   An artificer's artifice
> Mingling grace with valor
>
> Two flares
> Rose explosion
> Like two breasts unbound
> Raising their nipples insolently
> HE KNEW HOW TO LOVE
>   what an epitaph

A poet in the forest
Gazes languidly
    His revolver on its safety catch
At roses dying of hope

By contemporary standards, the mild disjunctions of the lyric "Festival" do not hold much difficulty for the reader. The implied backstory is well within grasp. Nonetheless, the poem illustrates the peculiar, energizing, jigsaw-puzzle quality that results when transitions are removed, and when grammar is broken. The verbless second stanza, for example, leaves it to the reader to infer the associative sequence of sensory perception, simile, and morbid-erotic fantasy:

Two flares
Rose explosion
Like two breasts unbound
Raising their nipples insolently
HE KNEW HOW TO LOVE
        what an epitaph

"Negligence" is the description Shattuck uses for the style of Apollinaire and his friend Pierre Reverdy, implying a casual, deliberately unbuttoned representation of mind-in-motion. But another, distinct effect of this fractured, fragment style of such undertelling is to create a faint aura of *enigma*. The memory of a woman, the bomb's flare, the poet on the battlefield, the possibility of death—these images and themes hover in loose relation to one another—but how do they go together? The speaker's thoughts and feelings are implicitly sketched, but loosely, elusively arranged. All poems contain some interpretive openness, but here the absence of connectives leaves much to the individual reader's intuition. Such is one primary effect of collage and juxtaposition: less orchestration, more participation.

"Festival" is a poem in the romantic tradition—a spontaneous-seeming expression of the individual sensibility in a heightened state. Its orientation is psychological. In Apollinaire's "Monday in Christine Street" (whose title serves as context), the fragments issue not from a single speaker, but from multiple voices. This is what literary critics now call "polyvocal" or "heteroglossaic." Here the intention of the collage is not to record the associative process of an individual, but the mosaic of a swirling social milieu. An excerpt:

> Those pancakes were divine
> the water's running
> Dress black as her nails
> It's absolutely impossible
> Here sir
> The malachite ring
> The ground is covered with sawdust
> Then it's true
> The redheaded waitress eloped with a bookseller.
>
> A journalist whom I really hardly know
>
> Look Jacques it's extremely serious what I'm going to tell you
>
> Shipping company combine

These two poems by the same writer, so distinct in character, yet employing a common technique, make evident a principle for reading: that to understand a particular poem employing fracture, it is important to recognize the underlying intention. Very similar-looking poetic surfaces can be the manifestations of very different underlying aesthetics. In the case of the two Apollinaire poems, "Festival" uses fragment to mime an intensely subjective psychic process; in "Monday in Christine Street," fragment is used to simulate the vivacious disorderliness of social realities.

The possible deployments and effects of poetic fracture and juxtaposition are too manifold to name or know. Yet even so, some familiar employments of poetic fracture can be identified, each with an underlying premise and an intended effect. These are:

1) to imply psyche in extremity (psychological expressionism)
2) to render actual perceptual process (impressionism)
3) to simulate the fracture and disorder of modern experience

4) to emphasize the inadequacy of language
5) to pose the poem on the page as an improvisatory "open" verbal field of possible combinations

I. Fragment Used as Psychological Expressionism

It makes sense to begin with (or to continue, from "Festival") the familiar category of #1, the psychological, where so much American poetry has staked its claim for the last one hundred years. One common employment of fracture is to evoke a speaker's heightened psychological state—distress, or, in some cases, rapture. In this category, the prosody of fragment imitates the accelerated or disrupted stream of consciousness of fear, excitement, or illumination, a state of mind that makes grammatical convention impossible.

Katie Ford's use of a fractured style in the poem, "Last Breath in Snowfall," skillfully creates the effect of a speaker in a heightened state—we are left to deduce whether the state is anxiety, hysteria, or transport:

> I loved one person do you see the evergreen there in fog one
>   by one
> I was taught to withdraw first from him do you want to know
>   how the mind
>
> works under extreme cold ice forming on the eyelid or wind
>   thrown
> at me I felt every needle felt every breath I've seen a vision of
>   you I was told
>
> and disobedience in it in it nakedness you have not surren-
>   dered have not torn
> his letters liken yourself therefore to the messenger who broke
>   the tablets

Here the effect of collage is to render an emotive voice caught in the scrambled tumult of interior experience; Ford's use of run-on and enjambment amplifies the fractured effect—a mind in stress, or, as the poem glosses itself, "how the mind works under extreme cold," questioning and querying. That voice impressionistically represents the fluttering zigzag path of mental process. Ford's poem embodies Shattuck's aesthetic claim for the "authenticity" of fracture: its irregularities register the uncertainty and struggle of speaking. By violating the conventions of syntax and narrative, the style requires that the reader participate imaginatively in the narrative context of the poem, the reconstruction of both story and the speaker's state of mind.

Of course, this technique is not exclusively modern. The Roman literary critic Longinus, in his essay on the Sublime, endorses the use of fragment by poets to simulate the disordered consciousness of great excitement: "The words issue forth without connecting links and are poured out as it were, almost outstripping the speaker himself. . . . the lines, detached from one another, but nonetheless hurried along, produce the impression of an agitation. . . . This result Homer has produced by the omission of conjunctions." Longinus might well be describing Katie Ford's contemporary poem: the passionate agitation of a single speaker expressed through the tumbled-together pieces of a narrative.

II. Fragment Used as Perceptual Impressionism

Another familiar poetic style employing fragment is the mode of terse, compressed description-narration, a kind of shorthand of seeing. In the following passage by Gary Snyder, the omission of transition and explication creates an impression of lucid unfiltered perception, of consciousness as a camera. Here, the use of fragment acts to suppress the presence of a narrator. In this Luddite linguistic style, verbs are scarce; even most adjectives seem excessive: This section is from Synder's *Back Country*:

**"Trail Crew Camp at Bear Valley, 9000 Feet. Northern Sierra—
White Bone and Threads of Snowmelt Water"**

> Cut branches back for a day—
> trail a thin line through willow
> > up buckbrush meadows

                    creekbed for twenty yards
          winding in boulders
                        zigzags the hill
     into timber, white pine.

     gooseberry bush on the turns
     hooves clang on the riprap
                    dust brush, branches.
                    a stone
          cairn at the pass—
     strippt mountains hundreds of miles

     sundown went back
                        the clean switchbacks to camp.
          bell on the gelding,
          stew in the cook tent,
          black coffee in a big tin can.

Scoff cautiously at this kind of essentialism. Snyder's writing may seem austerely nondirective, even primitive in its technique, but is not as casual as it appears. "Trail Crew Camp" employs its sketchbook minimalist technique to capture and hold precisely in place a constellation of experience. As in the Asian tradition, spareness of detail and form suggests an underlying vision of the natural world in which human presence is not central, and in which the physical, not the intellectual, has primacy. Here the use of fragment effectively omits the personality and commentary of the speaker.

Allen Ginsberg, in Section II of his poem "Iron Horse," employs a more stroboscopic impressionism than Snyder, but one likewise dedicated to perceptual veracity, and equally content with leaving out transition. In Ginsberg's cinematic, "word-movie" method, allegedly adapted from Jack Kerouac's *On the Road* mode, we feel the rush to get-it-all-in, relevant to his urban subject matter. Though we may feel the excited consciousness of the speaker, the intention here is primarily mimetic, the registration of outward, not inward, perception.

Bus outbound from Chicago Greyhound basement
green neon beneath streets Route 94
Giant fire's orange tongues & black smoke
pouring out   that roof,
little gay pie truck passing the wall—
Brick & trees, E. London, antique attics
mixed with smokestacks
Apartments apartments square windows set like Moscow
apartments red brick for multimillion population
out where industries raise craned necks
Gas station lights, old old old old traveler

Perhaps the speed of Ginsberg's eye and mind is a kind of emulation of urban velocity—he is riding a Greyhound bus, after all. It makes a certain sense that Ginsberg sometimes cited as a model the rough brushwork of Cezanne, whose painterly intention was a less mediated, more "raw" perceptual flow.

III. Fragment Used to Imply the Fracture and Disorder of Modern Experience

Although Ginsberg's joyful "Iron Horse" descriptions suggest some of the dishevelment and disorders of the modern world ("antique attics / mixed with smokestacks"), that disorder is not its primary focus. Even so, the disordering welter of modern reality is the most commonly cited rationale for fragmentation of poetic styles. In fact, it is the most frequently offered explanation of postmodern art in general, and T. S. Eliot's *The Waste Land* is probably the most frequently cited example, as in this polyglot, collaged passage from the poem's very end:

Shall I at least set my lands in order?
London Bridge is falling down falling down falling down
Poi s'ascose nel foco che gli affina
Quando fiam uti chelidon—O swallow swallow
Le Prince d'Aquitaine à la tour abolie
These fragments I have shored against my ruins
Why then Ile fit you. Hieronymo's mad againe.

In Eliot's rendition of modern Babel, it is unclear whether the linguistic fragmentation represents that of the speaker's mind or of an entire civilization. The poem has been read both ways, many times, of course, a fact that emphasizes the inseparability of the psychological from the environmental.

Eighty years later, in the beginning of Carolyn Forché's poem "On Earth," we find a contemporary cousin to *The Waste Land,* a similarly splintered composition of modern derangement, a collage of transitionless speeches, whose implication, more deliberately even than in Eliot, is the wreckage of the modern world:

"*now* appears to us in a mysterious light"

"did this happen? could it have happened?"
"everything ahead of her clear for the rest of her life"

"*La terre nous aimait un peu je me souviens*"

"I try to keep from wanting the morphine. I pray with both
     hands"

"Lima, Alpha, Uniform, November, Charlie, Hotel, Echo,
     November, Alpha, Bravo, Lima, Echo. Pap. Lima, Charlie,
     Alpha, Zero, One. Acknowledge. Out."

"man and cart disappeared in the blast, but their shadows
     remained on the bridge"

"these diaries a form of weather"

(a future hinting at itself)
(all of this must remain)
(on illness, after radiation, a mysterious illness)
(something) whispering
(the sadness when a hand—)
—with the resistance of a corpse to the hands of the living—

"open the book of what happened"

"Open the book of what happened" Forché's speaker says; and "these diaries a form of weather," the implication being that only in a decentered kind of gathering, with the nonhierarchical randomness of diaries or weather, can the sprawling disaster of modern history be adequately suggested. Because the subject is too large for any one speaker, fragments are used to imply the speech of many persons. Here again, we note the occlusion of a narrative presence. Conventional presentation, the form suggests, would imply comprehension of the incomprehensible and closure of what cannot be enclosed. Whispered hints and vocal intimacies enter some of the bits, but they are unattached to any particularized authorial presence. The irregular puctuation further implies disorder. For Forché, the style of fragment, ironically, offers both more intimacy and a wider grasp than discursively handled facts.

IV. Fragment Used to Imply the Inadequacy of Language

To read "On Earth" is like spinning the dial of a shortwave radio: the poet's method is to glean from the welter of voices and data. Yet in the Forché poem, even if modern history has unraveled our capacity to know it, there is still a faith in the naming power of language, in the fundamental pact between word and thing. That faith is not a presumption for the next category of fragment-slingers. In one quadrant of contemporary poetry, stutter, incompletion, and fragment are used to expose the inadequacies of language itself.

In some of Jorie Graham's work, for example, it is the inadequacy of language to name, the instability of language, the disconnect between sign and signified that takes the foreground. That shortcoming—represented by fragmented text—becomes the central subject matter of poetry:

Explain   door ajar.
Explain   hopeth all.
Explain   surface   future   subject-of.

Pierce.

Be swift.

(Let's wade again)

(Offstage: pointing-at)
(Offstage: stones placing themselves on eyes)

Here: tangle and seaweed

current   diagram   how deep? I have

forgotten.

(FROM "FOR ONE MUST WANT / TO SHUT
THE OTHER'S GAZE")

This Beckett-like excerpt comes from Graham's collection *Swarm*, a collection of poems in which a metaphysical distress is emblematized by a speaker at the end of speech. "Explain   hopeth all. / Explain surface future subject-of." Such broken speech implies a kind of semiotic shell shock, like a one-armed person poking the end of a thread at the eye of a needle that isn't there. If mad Ophelia had been a linguistic philosopher, she might have sung like this. The tone is one of tragic frustration.

These poetics near the end of speech have evolved their own vocabulary of technique; not just the stutter and the singular words floating on the page, but specialized punctuation, too: the blank ____; the empty parentheses ( ). Such subversive punctuation has its own implications. The blank, for instance, implies that the uttered is surrounded by the unsaid, or the unsayable. More generally, the implication might be that punctuation, which oversees connection-making like a traffic cop, is corrupt and dysfunctional. Whatever the intention, such irregular signage is another kind of fragmentation, with a similar insinuation.

Much contemporary poetry includes *some* acknowledgment of the limited capacity of words to stand for things. Inchoateness, like that of "For One Must Want / to shut the Other's Gaze," is an extremist mode of acknowledging such limitations. The enigmatic title of Michael Palmer's poem, "'or anything resembling it'" similarly seems to claim the shortcomings of language as its central topic. As in the passage by Graham, the speaker here seems marooned, or exiled, in an inadequate symbolic universe, that of a language which does not exactly reach any shore. The poem begins:

> The hills like burnt pages
> Where does this door lead
>
> Like burnt pages
> Then we fall into something still called the sea
>
> A mirrored door
> And the hills covered with burnt pages
>
> With words burned into the pages
> The trees like musical instruments attempt to read
>
> Here between idea and object
> Otherwise a clear even completely clear winter day

Despite the intrinsic intellectuality of such an enterprise, Palmer fashions his broken speech into a kind of existentialist lyricism. And here, again, fragments serve the poetic intention well: the short, abrupt units of speech emphasize that meaning is a brief, effortful, and somewhat stunted achievement.

In these two examples we can also discern that, even in such a minimalist, discontinuous style, different poetic speakers are nevertheless perceptibly distinct in tone. Graham's skittish and agitated style emphasizes the psychic plight of the individual speaker. Palmer's blunter and more composed speaker seems to speak of a collective human condition.

V. Fragment Used to Create the Poem as an "Open" Verbal Field of Possible Combinations

Perhaps these categories make it possible to identify some of the common underlying premises of fragment-using styles. To recognize a poet's emotional or intellectual intention is to possess a context that enables us as readers to better respond. But there are a thousand kinds, degrees, and styles of poetic disjunction. Despite the usefulness of categories, in the blurry hybridities of aesthetic practice, many contemporary poems fall outside any designated bin. In their multiple shifting dimensions, such poems often slide or jump-cut between different textures and agendas. Our ideas about what a fractured poem is "doing" at a given moment may inevitably be, to use Marjorie Perloff's famous term, "indeterminate."

This inconclusiveness of affect and content is precisely the desired effect of some poetry employing collage. Such poems would constitute our fifth, rather catchall hybrid category: poems that aren't specifically psychological or descriptive; not exclusively about modernity or the failure of language, but that are mainly compositions about the play of suggestiveness, without intending resolution. Such poetry celebrates the recombinant "openness" of its possible readings. We might call such poetry "experimental," though this label may not be of much help. The old term "open poetry" might be more appropriate.

Listen to the gusto of Jerome Rothenberg in his 1977 manifesto-essay, "New Models, New Visions," praising the poetry of "open forms."

> The action hereafter is "between" and "among," the forms
> hybrid and vigorous and pushing always toward an actual
> and new completeness. Here is the surfacing . . . of "fruit-
> ful chaos". . . . It is . . . the consequence in art-and-life of the
> freeing-up of the "dialectical imagination."

And here is the more contemporary, equally upbeat poet-critic Charles Bernstein, pitching the same product in more latter-day jargon:

> The moment not subsumed into a schematic structure, . . .
> but at every juncture creating (synthesizing) the structure. . . .
> Structure that can't be separated from decisions made within
> it, constantly poking through the expected parameters. . . .

Textures, vocabularies, discourses, constructivist modes of radically different character are not integrated . . . [but] constantly crisscrossing, interacting, creating new gels.

A representative sample of this orientation of collage-poetics can be found in the opening of "Tincture of Pine" by the poet Gillian Conoley. Conoley relishes wide gaps of association and uses the "field" of the page, à la Apollinaire, to hang fragments in the white space, "open" to the reader's interpretative industry:

I am Citizen of the wind,   I am bird-infested

Data and regret,   the clouds purl two

                              unhitch

                         [why only one head, why only

two faces]

one for noontide   one for old horse in the mire

Furious are giants arguing over maps

History lays a violence under the peacefulness,
someone goes
driving the car

Conoley's style here reminds us of some of the elemental premises and properties of most fragment and collage—its improvisatory freedom, its rough physicality on the page. These are properties that attracted the pioneers of modern poetry, William Carlos Williams, T. S. Eliot, and Ezra Pound. Here words are handled partly as manipulable physical materials; this aesthetic is sometimes known by the terms "constructivist" or "objectivist." The poem can be seen as a sort of mobile sculpture, one that may contain theme or narrative, but that also aspires to be an interesting object in its own right.

Yet Conoley's poem also reminds us of the dissatisfaction we can feel when meeting art of such jazzy freedom, poetry "without commitment to explicit syntactical relations between elements," as David Antin says. If a certain amount of inexplicitness is energizing, as we have seen, how "inexplicit" can a poem be and still give reader-gratification? How strong is our internal demand, as readers, for recognition of the form of what we are looking at? If we interrogate the poem using that criteria of recognition, we might ask, into which of our categories does "Tincture of Pine" fall? One argument could be made for category #1, the psychologically fractured. Likewise, there is evidence for category #4, the modernity-dissociated. The truth is probably some of each.

Yet even if we can contextualize "Tincture of Pine" by ascribing to it a predominant intention, does it give us enough distinct pleasure or entertainment, beauty or truth? Is Conoley's poem richly loose, like the "uncut," director's-version of the mind, or is it formless, like an unassembled puzzle? If poetry is an art of *concentration,* can it actually survive such *dispersedness* of content and form? If it is an art of *suggestiveness,* is this suggestive enough to reward our effort? These are some of the traditional controversies elicited by the collage-poem. To engage in its practice is necessarily to encounter the politics of completeness and partiality, mimesis, psychology, modernity, and deconstructive theory.

The poetry of fragment celebrates the connective resourcefulness of the human mind and the myriad simultaneous complexities of experience. It walks the balance beam between orientation and disorientation, between suggestiveness and mystification. Contemporarily, in some poetic circles, fracture and breakage have become the techniques by which authenticity and energy is certified—perhaps not much differently from the way in which explicit confession was once used in the past to certify poetic authenticity.

Yet if we can admire the variety of functions made possible by fragment and collage, we might also remember the considerable traditional powers that are foregone when a writer gives up the grammatical sentence: the complex powers of hierarchy and coordination, of flow, momentum, relativity, and precision.

As an example, we might look at the beginning of Allen Grossman's wild and weird narrative-meditative poem, "The Piano Player Explains Himself."

> When the corpse revived at the funeral,
> The outraged mourners killed it; and the soul
> Of the revenant passed into the body
> Of the poet because it had more to say.
> He sat down at the piano no one could play
> Called Messiah, or The Regulator of the World,
> Which had stood for fifty years, to my knowledge,
> Beneath a painting of a red-haired woman
> In a loose gown with one bared breast, and played
> A posthumous work of the composer S——
> About the impotence of God (I believe)
> Who has no power not to create everything.
> It was the Autumn of the year and wet,
> When the music started. The musician was
> Skilled but the Messiah was out of tune
> And bent the time and the tone. For a long hour
> The poet played The Regulator of the World
> As the spirit prompted, and entered upon
> The pathways of His power—while the mourners
> Stood with slow blood upon their hands
> Astonished by the weird processional
> And the undertaker figured his bill.

Grossman's fabular poem operates within the laws of storytelling, description, and grammar. Yet it gathers up vivid handfuls of the world into its ample subordinate clauses, while plunging forward in its discursive story, rhythmically and syntactically gaining momentum and grandeur, while implementing a provocative medley of tones and themes. Here, transition and the inherited conventions of complex grammar seem to permit wildness, not to curtail it. The narrative offers plentiful opportunities for the reader's mind to go sideways, to speculate, to "fill in," and yet the coherence of this created world gives it depth and invites the reader to invest imagination and emotion. We could call this a landscape that is inflated, not collapsed; three dimensional, not two-; explicit, not implied. It does not expose the structures of meaning, but uses them to increase the store of available reality. The powers of complex coherence, visible in Grossman's poem and available to all of us, shouldn't be lightly abandoned, or shunned.

In an essay called "Fragments and Ruins" Frank Kermode offers us some words that might lend us a place to close in a suggestive, rather than a definitive, way: "we can reasonably say that over the philosophy or propaganda of the fragment there broods inescapably the shadow of totality." Kermode also quotes the German philospher Friedrich Schlegel:

To have a system, that is what is fatal for the mind; not to have one, this too is fatal.

Thingitude and Causality

IN PRAISE OF MATERIALISM

Step out onto the Planet.
Draw a circle a hundred feet round.

Inside the circle are
three hundred things nobody understands, and, maybe
nobody's ever really seen.

How many can you find?

—LEW WELCH

In New York I get into an empty hotel elevator and smell cigarette smoke. Someone has been breaking rules. Maybe tapping the ashes into the palm of his hand or catching them in the sleeve of the half-empty pack, trying to leave no evidence. Maybe it was the Jamaican night clerk, trying to stay awake at 5 A.M., or the short, leathery Irish nun I passed on the fourth floor. And someone else has left a ghost in this small room: a faint trace of lilac perfume. Those other lives, their little stories. And was the person wearing perfume the same as the one who smoked? To stand alone in the midday quiet on the frayed flowered carpet of the hotel elevator, descending like a spider on its black cable, is like a sweet secret I am finally in on.

It's not that I shunned the material world when I was younger. Rather, I hardly noticed it. The fierce bubbling of anxiety and desire tended to obstruct my view of the environment. When I was eighteen, I thought the world was what you stood on while you were having your identity crisis. I thought it was the place examples came from. I churned up plenty of experience, like a dirt bike charging up a muddy slope, but none of it seemed to stick. Finding out that the physical world was not a theory or a feeling was quite a shock for me.

In the salons of aesthetic theory, one long-standing postulate claims that postmodern conditions elicit and require radical artistic forms. When T. S. Eliot says, "These fragments I have shored against my ruins," one way we understand it is, "Fragmented self + fragmented world= fragmented poem." In order to be legitimate and adequate, the assumption goes, modernist poetry should incorporate confusion into its means or its ends.

Largely, I subscribe to this standardized description of modern experience. My personal sense of self is that of barely manageable wreckage. Likewise, the contemporary civilized world feels to me like a wild, disparate, disorganized cascade of data, merchandise, noise, stimuli, selves—quite horrible in its volume, if not its particulars.

Yet it is precisely my own private, internalized "postmodernity"— my short attention span, my rootless life, my neural disarray, my ruins and fragments—that has led me, increasingly, to value the material world in poems. As a younger reader, I loved poems that bent and disassociated this world, this world that only pretended to be sensible and neat. I hated the poetics of realism because of the ways it seemed to confine and oppress possibility. Having no distance from immediate experience I only desired to escape it. Now I crave information and arrangement; I like to read nonfiction prose, and I love poems that locate, coordinate, and subordinate, that build up a compound picture of the world. These poetic properties—of attention, proportion, and relationality—I have come to think of as Thingitude and Causality.

Perhaps this is a matter of taste, or the encroaching conservatism of age, but I don't entirely believe that my shift in preference is just personal. I think it has been a matter of instinct, the way the body senses a vitamin deficiency and craves tomatoes or cauliflower. The environment—by which I mean life in a first-world culture at the start of the twenty-first century—is so corrupted, distorted, so informationally dense, and so disconnected, it elicits a longing for perspective. When I look around me I see a whole population of young poets who also seem disconnected, who are operating in the realm of conceptual excitement and linguistic fabrication, their flags planted in the seemingly endless fertility of self, poetical theory, and manic invention. To them I would advocate more Thingitude and Causality.

Let me give an example of the sort of thing I mean, like this excerpt from Brenda Hillman's poem "Fortress," a passage that thrills me with the lucidity, the particularity, and comprehension of its looking;

I. Night Watchman

August, the season of mild excess,
and the moon comes out like a rumor;
the night watchman stands on the avenue,

weaponless,
kicking one low black shoe with the other
while people go in and out of the liquor store.

There is a row of bottles behind him like bowling pins,
a cashier smoking beside the jars of olives,
and a tall cardboard man in a tuxedo, holding a martini,

and colorful refrigerated items with halved, sweating fruit;

but the night watchman is sober and short,
his crooked badge has numbers and a floral wreath,

his whole body blocks the doorway
as he hums a greeting at the regulars
who have come out, in desperation, at midnight.

Hillman's description brims with sensibility, but the sensibility has not obstructed or abstracted the lucidity of the seeing. Ideas infiltrate this scene like groundwater—the link between consumerism and despair, for instance—but it is the Seen that occupies the poetic stage. Restraint of the self in deference to the world is part of a representational ethic here; ideas must settle for a supportive, unobtrusive—even if shaping—role. Understandings are surely here, but they are not the primary material. Or, to put it another way, as W. C. Williams suggested, the dialectics of the poem are represented in the particulars, not the commentary.

But wait, you say—this argument is not just antiquarian, but utterly unnecessary. Don't all poems have some allegiance to things? What poem doesn't believe in the noun, which is the written residence of the thing? Well, consider the opening of John Ashbery's poem "Notes from the Air":

A yak is a prehistoric cabbage: of that, at least, we may be
     sure.
But tell us, sages of the solarium, why is that light
still hidden back there, among the house-plants and rubber
     sponges?
For surely the blessed moment arrived at midday

and now in mid-afternoon, lamps are lit,
for it is late in the season. And as it struggles now
and is ground down into day, complaints
are voiced at the edge of darkness: look, it says,

it has to be this way and no other.

Ashbery's charming style of floating talk is discursive and figurative, but even when things are named, one senses their status as that of place-holders in a verbal fabrication; things in Ashbery are usually weightless, blown about on the gusts of his rhetorical improvisation. Such a poem is more interested in exploring the constructions of meaning than in arranging a grid of experience through which we might know the world. Or rather, an Ashbery advocate might say, it is not the objective, but the experience of psychological flow that the poem emulates and simulates.

In other words, there are many different distances from thingitude, many relative degrees of physicality and rarification. God bless Ashbery for including a yak, a cabbage, and a solarium, but in "Notes of the Air," these words are relatively free of content. They are not entities in the great chain of being, but dialectics of diction in a poem; pigments employed by the artist for sake of balancing the color scheme. When it comes to reference, Ashbery's nouns don't bring the outside *in*; they turn the outside inside-out.

A loyalty to materialism is not the same thing as back-to-basics schooling or an austere fundamentalism. Poetic thingitude can be verbally acrobatic, flashy and energetic. An interest in the world and its anatomy does not condemn a poem to representational asceticism, or photorealism, or functional plainness, like Shaker furniture. After all, poetry drawn from the world has the advantage of a bottomless resource. It can import wholesale from the manifold known. It can also reflect and gratify our collective hunger for recognition; to see our world. This is much the case with the opening of Adrian Blevins's "Kings of the Trampoline." Blevins's voice is vernacular, alive and curious, but she also understands the fascination of the real:

> The story of the woman who'd been shot in the neck in the
>   Texaco
> got straight away complicated by the story of how I was hear-
>   ing it
>
> with a baby on my hip. Then the story of how she bled to
>   death
>
> on the very spot I happened to be standing
> with a pack of cigarettes and a tiny cherry sucker the color of
>   a nipple
>
> got complicated by the picture-book story of the pig Olivia
>
> from *Olivia Saves the Circus,* since the baby and I went right
>   home

to read it. Olivia paints Jackson Pollocks on the living room
     wall

and lies about being Queen of the Trampoline to her teacher,

Street violence, nipple-colored suckers, politically incorrect smoking moms, childrens' books, and the paintings of Jackson Pollock; all
are part of the thingitudinous swirl of Blevins's universe, and they
are all strung together in the sticky, extensive syntax of the narrative.
Though the reader doesn't know where this poem is going, we can
feel the momentum that nouns gather simply by their combination;
the things themselves are a tone and a story.

With the Blevins example, we see the lyric moment sprawling out
over its perimeter into the past and future; in other words, time is
part of the picture—a sense of the sequence of things. Though the
speaker herself doesn't pretend to know *how* things are related, she
knows that they *are;* their proximity in time and space means that
they affect each other. When things are connected not just by association, but coordinated in sequences of cause and effect, the vision of
the world increases in complexity and in import. This consciousness
of causality can increase the comprehensiveness of poems, and such
poems, when well done, carry a credential of worldliness that other
poems are hard pressed to match.

Causality is at work when the poetic vision includes not just the
luminous and particular present moment, but antecedents and consequences. Such a vision of the world springs from a different kind of
aesthetic instinct than the merely perceptual. One way to put it is that
the poet's vision becomes less rapturously preoccupied by Being and
more mindful of the sequences of Happening, of the ways in which
reality is shaped by its histories and its contexts. The world is subject
to systems, and the parts of the world are bound by those systems,
no matter how numinous they may be in singularity. W. S. Merwin's
poem "Native" shows this kind of deep consciousness of what stories
underlie the sensory facts of the present:

Most afternoons
of this year which is written as a number

in my own hand
on the white plastic labels

I go down the slope
where mules I never saw
plowed in the sun and died
while I was in school

they were beaten to go
straight up the hill
so that in three years the rain
had washed all the topsoil

out past sea cliffs
and frigate birds
only a few years
after the forest were gone

now I go down past
a young mango tree
to the shelves made of wood
poisoned against decay

there under a roof
of palm fronds and chicken wire
I stare at the small native plants
in their plastic pots
. . . .

here seeds from destroyed valleys
open late
beside their names in Latin
in the shade of leaves I have put there

Merwin's poem is rich with the panoramas of chronology, the dialectics of things in time. To single out just one example, consider the
ironic-historical coagulate embodied by the endangered native plants—
ancient, almost extinct species, growing in twentieth-century plastic

pots, labeled with their Latin names, and resting on the preservative-poisoned wood of the shelf. It's not that Merwin is telling what we usually think of as a "narrative"; it's that he has a deep and cultivated sense of manifold causalities and consequences that are lodged inside any moment. His vision of the double and tripleness of what is before us makes the complex resonance of the poem's present. The poet here fulfills the roles of both bard and seer: he is a storyteller and an usher into mystery.

Alan Shapiro, in a wonderful essay, "In Praise of the Impure," which redefines and champions the narrative instinct in poetry, describes the instinct behind a poem such as Merwin's, a poem whose vision looks backward and forward as well as at the present:

> the life of narrative begins with the desire to move between
> states of feeling so as to understand and articulate the com-
> munity of relations which obtains when the poet asks why, as
> well as how, he feels. . . . Narrative arises with the recognition
> that we are bearers of history. . . . embedded in the various
> traditions we inherit and transform. . . .

Shapiro's idea of the "community of relations" that poetry might articulate is a broad one, one that allows for a great variety of styles and temperaments. The poems of the French poet Jean Follain are technically lyric, not narrative, but they possess the charisma of both Thingitude and Causality. His poetry blends both a strong instinct for objectivity and a fluid mystical rapture. His poems are song-like, but almost always have a dash of narrative in them. Follain combines the stillness of seeing with the connectedness of story. Often, as in his poem "Death," Follain focuses on the histories of things as they flow through human lives. Reading such a poem, we are given a lucid sense of how the world is linked in time: from antecedents, to events, to aftermaths:

> From the bones of animals
> the factory had made these buttons
> which fastened

a bodice over the bust
of a gorgeous working-girl
when she fell
one of the buttons came off in the night
and the water of the gutters took it
and laid it down
in a private garden
with a crumbling plaster statue
Pomona
naked and laughing.

This magical vignette in thirteen lines is full of mystery, but also of hierarchies and orders. The realms of gods, humans, and animals are all subject to, and linked by, the laws of eros and death. In this world, the lives of animals are sacrificed for the beauty of girls. A girl's beauty in turn contributes to her fall. That "fall" (which may be sexual, or mortal, or both) is witnessed by the laughing naked mythic figure of Pomona (a reclusive virgin), who is both outside of time and herself disintegrating. In this world, the poem lets us know, some things happen in factories, and some things happen in secluded gardens. The individual stories of before, during, and after are fascinating, tragic, and divine; in the context of each other, they become even more so.

There are many kinds of poem in the universe, and room for them, but poems like those praised here bring the world to me and bring me to the world. I have a personal stake in the function they fulfill. If I sometimes go to poetry for its disorientations, what Rimbaud called the "derangement of the senses," at other times I value its ability to tell me a version that "makes" sense, a version whose wondrousness arises from the recognition of systems.

Modern consciousness may indeed be splintered, but it is one function of poetry in our time to fasten it back together—which does not mean to deny its complexity. When poetry can name the parts and position them, when it brings us out of the speedy, buzzing fog that is selfhood and modern life, our sense of being alive is heightened and intensified. How strange it is that when I read a particular poem, which brings the world into focus for me, that I can feel my own self come into focus. I was already part of that world, I know—but the unifying, clarifying impact of the poem delivers me to a deeper, and more conscious state of being-in-the-world. Deeper and better than before, when I was only lost in it.

Fear of Narrative and the
Skittery Poem of Our Moment

Aesthetic shifts over time can be seen as a kind of crop rotation; the topsoil of one field is allowed to rest, while another field is plowed and cultivated. In the 1970s, the American poetry of image covered the Midwestern plains like wheat; in the 1980s, perhaps, it was the narrative-discursive sentence that blossomed and bore anthological fruit. This shifting of the ground of convention is one aspect of cultural self-renewal. But the fruitful style and idiom become conventional and then, conventionally tired.

Since the 1990s, American poetry has seen a surge in associative and "experimental" poetries, in a wild variety of forms and orientations. Some of this work has been influenced by theories of literary criticism and epistemology, some by the old Dionysian imperative to jazz things up. The energetic cadres of MFA graduates have also contributed to this milieu, founding magazines, presses, and aesthetic clusters that encourage and influence one another's experiments. Generally speaking, this time could be characterized as one of great invention and playfulness. Simultaneously, it is also a moment of great aesthetic self-consciousness and emotional removal.

Systematic development is out; obliquity, fracture, and discontinuity are in. Especially among young poets, there is a widespread mistrust of narrative forms, and, in fact, a pervasive sense of the inadequacy or exhaustion of all modes other than the associative. Under the label of "narrative," all kinds of poetry currently get lumped misleadingly together: not just story, but discursion, argument, even descriptive lyrics. They might better be called the "Poetries of Continuity."

Let me begin with two poetic examples that I think intriguingly register one aspect of the current temper—mistrust of narrative. The first is from "Couples" by Mark Halliday:

> All the young couples in their compact cars.
> He's funny and she's sensible.
> The car is going to need some transmission work
> soon, but they'll get by all right—
> Aunt Louise slips them a hundred dollars
> every chance she gets and besides,
> both of them are working—
> Susan does day-care part-time
> and Jim finally got full-time work
> at Design Futures Associates
> after those tough nine months as an apprentice.
> Or he's in law school
> doing amazingly well, he acts so casual
> but really he's always pounding the books,
> and Susan works full-time
> for a markets research firm, she's
> amazingly sharp about consumer trends
> and what between her salary and Aunt Louise
> Jim can afford to really concentrate on
> his studies. Or he's a journalist
> and so is she, and they keep very up
> on the news especially state politics.
> Plus she does an amazing veal marsala

and he jogs two miles five mornings a week—
and in June they'll be off to Italy again,
or Mexico; Susan's photographs are
really tasteful, not touristy, she always
reads up on the culture before their trip.
Jim slips in a wacky shot every once in a while
and everybody laughs, that's old Jim.
. . . .
They'll get by all right. They have
every one one of Linda Ronstadt's albums, and
they're amazingly happy together,

The second poem is "First Person Fabulous" by Matthea Harvey:

First Person fumed & fizzed under Third Person's tongue while
Third Person slumped at the diner counter, talking, as usual, to
no one. Third Person thought First Person was the toilet paper
trailing from Third Person's shoe, the tiara Third Person once
wore in a dream to a funeral. First Person thought Third Person
was a layer of tar on a gorgeous pink nautilus, a foot on a fountain, a tin hiding the macaroons & First Person was that nautilus, that fountain, that pile of macaroons. Sometimes First
Person broke free on first dates (with a Second Person) & then
there was the delicious rush of "I this" and "I that" but then no
phone call & for weeks Third Person wouldn't let First Person
near anyone. Poor First Person. Currently she was exiled to the
world of postcards (*having a lovely time*)—& even then that
beast of a Third Person used the implied "I" just to drive First
Person crazy. She felt like a television staring at the remote,
begging to be turned on. She had so many things she wanted
to say. If only she could survive on her own, she'd make Third
Person choke on herself & when the detectives arrived & all
eyes were on her, she'd cry out, "I did it! I did it! Yes, dahlings,
it was me!"

These two ingenious poems, written by poets of different generations (Halliday, fifty-something, Harvey, thirty-something) and styles,

have something strikingly in common: their intention to hold narrative up for our inspection, at arm's length, without being caught inside its sticky web. Rather than narratives themselves, both poems offer commentaries about narrative, story "samples," safely told by a narrator who operates at an altitude above plot, narrating from a supervisory position. You could truly say that these poems serve to sharpen our awareness of our narrative habits, but you could also say they contain a warning about how generic, how overfamiliar, our storytelling is.

Halliday's poem "Couples" seems to make the point that our most precious personal narratives, despite our tender feelings for them, are generic—that human beings (yuppie couples, at least) are reducible to socioeconomic-historic clichés—no matter that we cling to the idea of our uniqueness and individuality. These stories of the self, the poem makes clear, are an exhausted resource.

Harvey's ingenious, funny poem trumps the problem by translating the plot into a drama between Signifiers, transposing Drama into Grammar. Her poststructural poem implies that most storytelling (and maybe psychology itself) is structured by grammar. The ironic title, "First Person Fabulous," suggests the essential egotism of all first-person narratives. Tender and witty though the poem is about its "characters," a real involvement by the reader is prevented by the latex condom of self-consciousness. Harvey's poem is representative of the strategic ingenuity of the new poetry, but "First Person Fabulous" is a poem, we are never allowed to forget, about pronouns.

It seems important to point out that both of these poems, though intrinsically skeptical, are also markedly playful. In their inventiveness of detail, in their teasing, in-and-out, back-and-forth development, in their pleasure in idiom, they are not cold in their detachment, but imaginatively frolicsome. In fact, the self-consciousness of the poems creates the verbal dimension in which they play. However, despite the affirmative, vital presence of imagination, that playground area is situated at a great distance from experience. It is distinctly externalized. *Distance* is as much the distinctive feature of the poems as play; distance that might be seen as antithetical to that other enterprise of poetry—strong feeling.

What aspect of narrative, with which these poems flirt, in their ironical skeptical ways, is so to be guarded against? A number of familiar explanations present themselves. To start with, it seems likely that narrative poetry in America has been tainted by its overuse in thousands of confessional poems. Not confessionalism itself, but the inadvertent sentimentality and narcissism of many such poems have imparted the odor of indulgence to narrative. Our vision of narrative possibilities has been narrowed by so many first-person autobiographical stories, then drowned in a flood of pathos-poems. Psychology itself, probably the most widely shared narrative of the last several generations of American culture, has lost its charisma as a system, if not its currency.

Secondly, many persons think that ours is simply not a narrative age; that contemporary experience is too multitracked, too visual, too manifold and simultaneous to be confined to the linearity of narrative, no matter how well done. As Carolyn Forché says,

> Our age lacks the structure of a story. Or perhaps it would be
> closer to say that narrative implies progress and completion.
> The history of our time does not allow for any of the bromides
> of progress, nor for the promise of successful closure.

Forché herself is an aesthetic convert from narrative poetry to a poetry of lyric-associative fragment.

Not only is organized narration considered inadequate to contemporary experience; its use is felt by some to be oppressive, overcontrolling, "suspiciously authoritarian." Because narrative imposes a story upon experience, because—the argument goes—that story implicitly presents itself as the *whole* story, some readers object to the smugness and presumption of the narration. "Whose narrative is this?" they cry. "Not mine!"

Put more bluntly, the new resistance to conventions of order represents a boredom with, and generalized suspicion of, straightforwardness and orchestration. Systematic development and continuity are considered simplistic, claustrophobic, even unimaginative. In the contemporary arena of the moment, charisma belongs to the erratic and subversive.

There may be yet another, more hidden and less conscious anxiety behind the contemporary mistrust of narrative: a fear of submersion, or enclosure. Narrative, after all, and other poetries of sustained development seduce and contain. Its feature is the loss of self-consciousness; in the sequential "grip" of narrative, the reader is "swept away," and loses, not consciousness perhaps, but self-consciousness. The speedy conceptuality that characterizes much contemporary poetry prefers the dance of multiple perspectives to sustained participation. It hesitates to enter a point of view that cannot easily be altered or quickly escaped from. It would prefer to remain skeptical, and in that sense, too, one might say that it prefers knowing to feeling.

I offer these two initial poem-examples as manifestations of one kind of hip contemporary skittishness. But Harvey and Halliday, though subversive in their ways, are too reader friendly, too lucid and inclusive to truly represent the poetic fashion of the moment. "Couples" and "First Person Fabulous" are not the epicenter poems of the moment. The predominant Poem of Our Moment is actually a more lyric and disassociative thing. Here is one example by poet Rachel M. Simon—snappy, jump-cutting, witty, and abstract.

Improvisation

One thing about human nature is that nobody
wants to know the exact dimensions of their small talk.
I can't imagine good advice.
If every human being has skin
how come I can see all of your veins?
Clicks and drips target my skull.
Important voices miss their target.
Some cities are ill-suited for feet.
I'd never buy a door smaller than a tuba, you never know
what sort of friends you'll make.
In the future there will be less to remember.
In the past I have only my body and shoes.
The gut and the throat are two entirely different animals.
My hands don't make good shoelaces, but I'm going to stay
in this lane, even if it's slower.
The trick was done with saltwater and smoke
and an ingredient you can only find in an
out of business ethnic food store.

It all comes down to hand-eye coordination.
Once it took all of my energy to get you out of the tub
we had converted from an indoor pool to a house.
I ended up on snorkeling spam lists inadvertently.
It is all inadvertent.
If you don't believe me ask your mom.

"Improvisation" is a quintessential poem of the moment: fast-moving and declarative, wobbling on the balance beam between associative and disassociative, somewhat absurdist, and, indeed, cerebral. Much talent and skill are evident in its making, in its pacing and management of gaps, the hints and sound bites that keep the reader reaching forward for the lynchpin of coherence. The formal stability of serial declaration, for example, is countered by the disjunctness of those declarations. "Improvisation" even contains its own self-description: "It is all inadvertent" is the process-metaphor of the poem, describing itself and the modern consciousness the poem embodies. One admirable aspect of the poem is the way it seems capable of incorporating anything; yet the correlative theme of the poem is that all this motley data—i.e., experience—*doesn't* add up to a story. Even as the poem implies a world without sequence, the poem itself has no consequence, no center of gravity, no body, no assertion of emotional value.

If we ask, What *is* the subject of "Improvisation," the answer would be, the dissociated self; and the aspect of self such poems most forcefully represent is its quicksilver uncatchability, its flittering, quicksilver transience. Poems like "Improvisation" showcase personality, in the persona of their chatty, free-associating, nutty-smart narrators. It is a self that does not stand still, that implies a kind of spectral, anxious insubstantiality. The voice is plenty sharp in tone and sometimes observant in its detail, but it is skittery. Elusiveness is the speaker's central characteristic. Speed, wit, and absurdity are its attractive qualities. The last thing such poems are going to do is risk their detachment, their distance, their freedom from accountability. The one thing they are not going to do is commit themselves to the sweaty enclosures of subject matter and the potential embarrassment of sincerity.

I don't wish to base a case on one example, so I will offer a few others. Here are the opening stanzas of two other recent poems, which could be characterized by their speed, wit, dislocation, and self-conscious oddity. The first is from "Watercooler Tarmac" by G. C. Waldrep:

My harvest has engineered a sanctioned nectary.
The transmission of each apple squeals when I apply the
    compress.
All my obsequities have finished their summer reading,
they are diligent students,
they understand the difference between *precision* and *Kansas.*
This was before I had pried up the floorboard to see
what was ticking underneath.
I keep busy, every plane that flies through my sky
requires help, sign language for the commercial vector.
My octave's intact so this may be working.

The second is "Variations as the Fell of the Fall" by Kevin McFadden:

Oily fellows, earthmen. Spell
freeway, spell monolith, sell
me a fossil. Wholly repellent.
Malls, only relief. Post. Wheel
wells, the atmosphere (lolly-
lolly) honest, simple welfare,
topsoil anywhere—fell smell,
fell smell. Weaponry, hostile
fish, watermelon peels (lolly-
lolly) parentheses, mile, wolf,
fearsome whelp. Listen (lolly-
lolly) stolen female whisper.
Hollow salesman trifle, yelp
then loll. Mayflower slip. See
ELSE. My free hilltop, all snow.
Frost. Meanwhile sleep (lolly-
lolly) meanwhile self. Presto!
Trill myself open wholesale!

Sure, these styles have discernable origins and different, respectable precedents. In "Watercooler Tarmac" and "Improvisation" we might see the cartoony goofiness of James Tate or the unmoored rhetoric of John Ashbery. In the more radical "Variations as the Fell of the Fall," one senses an aleatory nonsense-language system at work. Upon inspection, it turns out that every line in "Variations" is built from the same rearranged letters. Though these styles are different, they share the aesthetic principle of verbal-psychic dislocation. Likewise, they all move with a manic swiftness. What is also striking, to me, and representative of the aesthetic moment, is how these poems are committed to a sort of pushy exteriority; they may entertain, but they do not admit the reader.

Of course, dissociative doesn't necessarily mean detached, or empty, or even hyper-intellectual. "The Love Song of J. Alfred Prufrock" is one example of a dissociated yet passionate poem. In various poetic hands, the dissociated-improvisatory mode can represent vivaciousness of self, or uncontainable passion, or the fractured wash of modernity, or an aesthetic allegiance to randomness. The spirit of the poem—if we can recognize what it is—makes all the difference.

What are the intentions of the current version of "difficult" poetry? Some of the stated, advertised intentions of "elusive" poetics are to playfully distort or dismantle established systems of meaning, to recover mystery in poetry, to offer multiple simultaneous interpretive possibilities for the energetic and willing reader to "participate" in. The critic Stephen Burt describes some of the traits of this poetic style, for which he offers the term "Elliptical Poetry":

> Elliptical poets are always hinting, punning, or swerving away
> from a never-quite-unfolded backstory; they are easier to pro-
> cess in parts than in wholes. They believe provisionally in
> identities (in one or more "I" per poem), but they suspect the
> Is they invoke: they admire disjunction and confrontation, but
> they know how little can go a long way. Ellipticists seek the
> authority of the rebellious; they want to challenge their read-
> ers, violate decorum, surprise or explode assumptions about

what belongs in a poem, or what matters in life, and to do so while meeting traditional lyric goals.

Burt's definition is quite general—it has to be in order to encompass the mélange of poetry he champions—but he gets the mania and the declarativeness right. Also the relentless dodging or obstruction of expectation. Avante-gardes of the past have surely rejected linearity and conventions of coherence, but some of them did so with the motive of asserting worlds of feeling—amazement or distress—that could not be expressed within conventions of order. Consider the surrealism of Lorca, or Vallejo, which embraced both arbitrariness and passion with radical subjectivity. Yet surrealism operates out of a faith in psychic veracity, and surrealism has a heroic aspect to it. As Louis Aragon says, "the marvelous is born of the refusal of one reality, yet also of the development of a new relationship, of a brand new reality which this refusal has liberated." Here is Aragon's "Pop Tune," performed in a style quite congruent to "Improvisation," but with a larger, quite different motive:

Cloud
A white horse stands up
and that's the small hotel at dawn where he who is always
    first-come-first-served awakes in palatial comfort
Are you going to spend your entire life in this same world
Half dead
Half asleep
Haven't you had enough of commonplaces yet
People actually look at you without laughter
They have glass eyes
You pass them by you waste your time you pass away and
    go away
You count up to a hundred during which you cheat to kill an
    extra ten seconds
You hold up your hand suddenly to volunteer for death
Fear not
Some day
There will be just one day left and then one day more after that

Then that will be that
No more need to look at men nor their companion animals
    their Good Lord provides
And that they make love to now and then
No more need to go on speaking to yourself out loud at night
    in order to drown out
The heating-units lament
No need to lift my own eyelids
Nor to fling my blood around like some discus
Nor to breathe despite my disinclination to
Yet despite this I don't want to die
In low tones the bell of my heart sings out its ancient hope
That music I know it so well but the words
Just what were those words saying
"Idiot"

Aragon's bold, clownish poem, typical of this strain of French surrealism, is an exhortation to wonder. Its leaping, erratic movements
are meant to assert the urgency of the speaker, the range of human
nature, and the volatile resourcefulness of imagination.

The mention of death, the progressive intimacy of the voice, the
arrival at self-examination and tonal sincerity, all mark this as a poem
that combines rhetorical performance with interiority. "Life is hard"
the poem suggests, "time is unendurable and absurd, the sleep of
consciousness is oppressive, but it is still important to try to live."
Aragon's poem, for all its whimsy and dishevelment, is finally humanist, asserting values.

Narrated and associative poems are *not* each other's aesthetic op-
posites or sworn enemies. Obviously these modes don't necessarily
exclude each other. They overlap, coexist, and often cross-pollinate.
Nevertheless, one might truly say that the two modes call upon fun-
damentally different resources in reader and writer. Narration (and
its systematic relatives) implicitly honors Memory; the disassociative
mode primarily values Invention. "Poetries of continuity" in some
way aim to frame and capture experience; dissociative poetry verifies
itself by eluding structures. Their distinct priorities result in different poetries. A poetry that values clarity and continuity is obligated

to develop and deliver information in ways that are hierarchical and sequential, ways that accommodate and orchestrate the capacities of human memory. In contrast, a dissociative poetry is always shuffling the deck in order to evade knowability.

The Polish poet Czeslaw Milosz, whose well-known phrase, "the pursuit of the real," declares his allegiance in this matter, has something to say about organization in poems:

> . . . a poet discovers a secret, namely that he can be faithful to real things only by arranging them hierarchically. Otherwise, as often occurs in contemporary prose-poetry, one finds a "heap of broken images, where the sun beats," fragments enjoying perfect equality and hinting at the reluctance of the poet to make a choice.

Would it be so very inaccurate or unfair to say that poems like "Improvisation" or "Watercooler Tarmac," in the charming "democracy" of their dissociation, have a passive-aggressive relation to meaning? To say that, despite a certain charm, the coy ellipticism of these poems signifies a skepticism about the possibilities for poetic depth, earnestness, even about feeling itself?

These may seem like disproportionately heavy judgments to apply to a few playful butterfly poems fluttering by in the aesthetic breeze, but isn't their self-conscious lack of consequence part of the problem? Perhaps, in their deliberate intention to escape the confinement of one system they have also accidentally escaped another. Perhaps, in their effort to circumvent linearity, or logic, or obviousness, they have eluded representing anything but attitude—one of the familiar tendencies of modern American culture.

In contrast, to tell a story effectively, or to craft a persuasion, you have to decide what is important and arrange it so that the listener will grasp the grammar of the experience. In other words, you must orchestrate continuities, hierarchies, and transitions. Might we ask, finally—because it's good to remember as well as to go forward—what we lose when we jettison cohesion and continuity from our poetry? Perhaps as readers we lose the pleasure of security, the feeling of being seated deeply inside the poem, of progressing through a dramatic structure that accumulates and deepens, delays and delivers. Likewise, in reading a dissociative poem, we may also miss a kind of recognition, the resonance between experience and art that verifies them both. "The Geraniums," written fifty years ago by a forgotten poet, Genevieve Taggard, offers some of the pleasures of such habitation:

Even if the geraniums are artificial
Just the same,
In the rear of the Italian café
Under the nimbus of electric light
They are red; no less red
For how they were made. Above
The mirror and the napkins
In the little white pots . . .
. . . In the semi-clean café
Where they have good
Lasagne . . . The red is a wonderful joy
Really, and so are the people
Who like and ignore it. In this place
They also have good bread.

A simple poem, it would seem, "Geraniums" quietly dramatizes a scene that is particular, complex, and finely balanced. It is recognizably modern, too. Here, the man-made and the natural are confusingly bred into each other, pleasure is qualified but real, humans are inattentive. Consider, in the opening sentence, the four-line grammatical delay between the named subject (geraniums) and object (red), and the way the subsequent clause ("no less red / For how they were made") then lyrically reiterates and reverses the two paradoxical qualities of the flowers—their falseness and their beauty. The next sentence contains a similar extended delay and arrival that, when it comes, deepens and widens the speaker's conviction and her affection, emotionally emphasized by the modifiers "wonderful" and "really." Taggard's speaker is modest, quietly observant, engaged yet also editorial, measuring and asserting. This organized, hierarchical poem is a quiet joy. Its tone of speculative persuasion, deepening conviction, and even its ambivalence, is partly possible because of its stability, its grammar of relativity, its continuity. Is it oppressive for its closure, or boring for its clarity? Not to me. Instead, with lyrical dexterity, it manages both completeness and openness.

I keep wondering if we can identify a broader cultural explanation for the contemporary attraction to dissociation. Perhaps one reason is in our current, deeply ambivalent relation to knowledge itself.

We have yielded so much authority to so many agencies, in so many directions, that we are nauseous. When we go to a doctor, we entrust ourselves to his or her care blindly. When we see bombs falling on television, we assume someone else is supervising. We allow "experts" and "leaders" to make decisions for us because: 1) we already possess more data than we can manage, and 2) at the same time we are aware that we don't know enough to make smart choices. Forced by circumstances into this yielding of control, we are deeply anxious about our ignorance and vulnerability. It is no wonder that we have a passive-aggressive, somewhat resentful relation to meaning itself. In this light, the refusal to cooperate with conventions of sense-making seems like—and is—an authentic act of political, even metaphysical protest—the refusal to conform to a grammar of experience that is being debased by all-powerful public systems. This refusal was, we recall, one of the original premises of L=A=N=G=U=A=G=E poetry.

But when we push order away, when we celebrate its unattainability, when our only subject matter becomes instability itself, when we consider artful dyslexia and disarrangement as a self-gratifying end in itself, we give away one of poetry's most fundamental reasons for existing: the individual power to locate and assert value.

In one of the Lannan Foundation interviews, poet Robert Hass says, "It is wrong to have an elegiac attitude toward reality." Hass, in the context of that conversation, suggests that it is unethical to consider reality decisively outside the reach of language. To exclusively practice an art of which this is a premise and implication—that language is inadequate, that the word cannot reach the world—is a bad idea, one with a price tag attached.

This is a truly pluralistic moment in American poetry, one full of vitality as well as withdrawal. The palpable excitement in new poetry right now obviously answers a felt need, provides its own brand of nourishment. The sheer inventiveness abounding is extraordinary. But this might not be the wrong occasion to pronounce the word "fashion." Fashion is not in itself a negative force, but rather a perennial part of the vitality of culture. Fashion is the way that taste changes and then spreads, in a kind of swell or wave of admiration. *The Waste Land* was fashionable, and sideburns and Hemingway and war bonds and Sylvia Plath, and existentialism, and bell-bottoms. The danger in fashion is its lack of perspective, that it doesn't always recognize the deep structure of whatever manners it is adopting. Almost by definition, fashion can gather thoughtless followers. In his preface to the *Postmodern Poetry Anthology,* Paul Hoover acknowledges the potential for this trouble: "The risk is that the avant-garde will become an institution with its own self-protective rituals, powerless to trace or affect the curve of history."

One can understand how disassociative poetry has become fashionable, celebrated, taught, and learned—it is a poetry equal, in its velocity, to the speed and disruptions of contemporary culture. It responds to the postmodern situation with a joyful crookedness. And one can also see why poetics that assert sensible order (which, admittedly, *can* be predictable and reductive) have fallen a bit from fashion: after all, the pretense of order is, in some way, laughable. Art has to play, it has to break rules, to turn against its obligations, to be irresponsible, to recast convention. Some wildness is essential to its freedom. Yet every style has its shadowy limitation, its blind eye, its narcissistic cul-de-sac. There is a moment when a charming enactment of disorientation becomes an homage to dissociation. And there is a moment when the poetic pleasure of elusiveness, inadvertently, commits itself to triviality.

Fashion Victims

THE MISFORTUNES OF AESTHETIC FATE

What does it mean to come of age as an artist in a given era? Among other things, it means to be inducted into a period style, to accept certain aesthetic assumptions as truth, to have one and not another relationship to such elements as the sentence, sound, imagery, and tone.

All young poets are, to some extent, victims of fashion because young artists are by necessity imitators. To imitate is how one learns craft, and for young poets especially, art of the present moment exerts the greatest magnetism. Some are lucky to be born into an era whose style is coincidentally well suited to their talent and nature. Others are born into the wrong era, an artistic environment that clashes with their natural instincts.

For many poets of my generation, entering American poetry in the 1970s and '80s meant indoctrination into the plain style and / or the confessional mode, a fundamentalism of straightforwardness and sincerity. We inherited or acquired an allergy to grandeur, flourish, and most special effects.

It was a style conceived in reaction to its own predecessors, New Critical irony and formalist verse. That revolution is well known, and can be represented by the figure and the poems of James Wright, a poet trained in formalism, who overthrew his formalist training in favor of a kind of essentialism. His poems are the ultimate in unpretentiousness:

I Was Afraid of Dying

Once,
I was afraid of dying
In a field of dry weeds.
But now,
All day long I have been walking among damp fields,
Trying to keep still, listening
To insects that move patiently.
Perhaps they are sampling the fresh dew that gathers slowly
In empty snail shells
And in the secret shelters of sparrow feathers fallen on the
    earth.

If that generation—W. S. Merwin and Wright and Adrienne Rich and others—threw off their inherited aesthetic harness, my generation happily harnessed itself to theirs. The virtues of that plain style were clarity and a faith in sincerity. Its one extravagance was the image—sometimes surreal, sometimes descriptive. The cost to many of us was metrical ignorance and rhetorical underdevelopment. What many of us did not understand was that the technical resources of metrical writing gave access to kinds of poetic power that the plain style could almost never attain. In a way, we were like a tribe—the Plain Stylists—born into a remote village of simple homemade huts; we used wooden tools and ate nuts and berries. It took us years to recognize that our resources were less adequate than we had believed. We had the Confessional permission to be sensational, to mount frontal assaults on this or that, but we simply didn't have the technology to write lines like these, by Wallace Stevens:

A long time that you have been making the trip
From Havre to Hartford, Master Soleil,
Bringing the lights of Norway and all that.

(FROM "OF HARTFORD IN A PURPLE LIGHT")

Or like these, by John Donne:

In what torn ship soever I embark,
That ship shall be my emblem of thy Ark;
What sea soever swallow me, that flood
Shall be to me an emblem of thy blood;

(FROM "A HYMN TO CHRIST AT THE
AUTHOR'S LAST GOING INTO GERMANY")

Some contemporary practitioners of the plain style have had the genius to achieve remarkable power within its confines. Louise Glück and Louis Simpson are two notable examples. Their distinctive achievements have a lot to do with their mastery of understatement and the subtlest inferences of tone. They taught themselves to do more with less. Yet I've come to feel that many others of my tribe, myself included, were marooned on the small aesthetic island of the plain style. Sure, it seemed like a good idea at the time, and you might say that we chose it for ourselves, but did we really know enough then to make such a choice? And the fact is, once such definitive aesthetic choices are made by a writer, it is very hard to unmake them.

The message or moral is this: every period style has its sometimes invisible price tag. Time makes inherent limitations conspicuous. Arrested development is the rule, not the exception. Nonetheless, the book of individuation is never entirely shut. The diligent, the lucky, the insightful—those are the artists who continue to search both inside and outside the period style for more power, more sound, more adventure. If they experience a conflict between the received style and their own natures, or their potential, they will turn away from fashion; they will betray the teachings they once received as gospel and transform.

Negative Capability

HOW TO TALK MEAN AND INFLUENCE PEOPLE

> *I never turned anyone into a pig.*
> *Some people are pigs; I make them*
> *look like pigs.*
>
> *I'm sick of your world*
> *that lets the outside disguise the inside.*
> —"CIRCE'S POWER," LOUISE GLÜCK

Meanness, the very thing that is unforgivable in human social life, in poetry is thrilling and valuable. Why? Because the willingness to be offensive sets free the ruthless observer in all of us, the spiteful perceptive angel who sees and tells, unimpeded by nicety or second thoughts. There is truth-telling, and more, in meanness.

Take, for example, the W. C. Williams poem "The Last Words of My English Grandmother," a narrative of almost documentary objectivity.

> There were some dirty plates
> and a glass of milk

beside her on a small table
near the rank, disheveled bed—

Wrinkled and nearly blind
she lay and snored
rousing with anger in her tones
to cry for food,

Gimmee something to eat—
They're starving me—

Williams is mean here in the sense of *minimal*—this scene is un-dressed, un-spin-doctored. Left on our own, without the narrator's managerial help—without a tone, or backstory, or a confidential commentary—we are stuck as uncomfortable witnesses to human ugliness. If anything, there is, perhaps, the slightest edge of contempt implicit in the scene: the unlovely reality of the old woman, and of her evident neglect, do not speak kindly of human nature. And, since the title tells us that the old woman is the speaker's grandmother, he, too, is implicated. Williams's stoical style perfectly serves the drama of contesting wills that emerges, and the ruthless truth about power at the poem's center:

Let me take you
to the hospital, I said
and after you are well

you can do as you please.
She smiled, Yes
you do what you please first
then I can do what I please—

There is truth-telling in meanness, but that is not all of it. Meanness is also an aesthetic asset for its flavor of danger. Nothing wakes us up like menace—menace refreshes. When a poem becomes aggressive, it rouses an excitement in us, in part because we see that someone has broken their social shackles. We feel intoxicated by that outlaw freedom, and we covet it for ourselves. We also alertly intuit that we ourselves might be next on the hit list. Bad manners, we know, tend to be anarchic. At best, we will be caught flatfooted, left behind by the speed of the accelerating nastiness. At worst, we may find ourselves under attack.

What alertness we feel when Marianne Moore turns her scintillating gaze toward the second-person pronoun in lines 18 to 20 of "Critics and Connoisseurs": ". . . I have seen this swan and / I have seen you; I have seen ambition without / understanding in a variety of forms."

That willingness to make the occasional stabbing motion gives Moore's poems some of their great vigor. A wizard of tone, she is expert at floating vaguely ominous abstractions, and it gives her work an unpredictable edge that keeps us intent on following the progress of her fierce abstract sutures. She motivates us to pay attention. Moore is always assertive, but she is not always aggressive—and some of her poems suffer for it. "The Mind is an Enchanting Thing," one of her most-anthologized poems, suffers from too little ruthlessness, with its Mary Poppins tone and imagery of butterfly wings. If that poem were more tart, it would better represent both the mind and Moore.

Meanness seems to heighten the powers of discrimination and the language such discrimination requires. Meanness is a sort of literary endorphin, an exhilarating glandular stimulant. Repression and expression are, after all, the great partners in poetry, and when suppressed truth comes out, it tends to burst forth with the energy of a firehose breaking through the compartments of social discretion. When it does, we gather at the disaster to gawk. Stephanie Brown, in her first-rate book, *Allegory of the Supermarket* (1998), is uncommonly interested in—and skilled at—the tones and uses of mean. Her poem, "Mommy Is a Scary Narcissist," whose title itself establishes a passive-aggressive spin of quadratic complexity, is a good example:

C'mon, I shouldn't need to mention blepharoplasty.
Her mauled face is a part of the shared horizon.
I don't need to mention the lift, the tuck, the lipo.
(A Trinity.)

The smile-ever-smiling is a part of the position.
This is Mommy's supposition:
Sexy. Sexy. Sexy. Everlasting and in high-tonus stance.
    Decisions
Belong to dads, men, boyfriends, bartenders, chance.

Mommy looks good when she prays in the chapel.
(Ferns, lush foliage, candles, rose petals, and flattering paints)
Harder than the other mommies. No one stays.
(She looks into the baptismal font deeply, passionately, and
    long.)
Mommy tries to love, Mommy tries to get a job.
Not very hard, the outside world knows that, but Mommy
    doesn't.

Brown's ability to be both subtle and brutal springs directly from her willingness to be unpleasant. It helps that she has a keen eye for culture and understands its continuity with selfhood. She knows that the "mauled face is a part of the shared horizon," but that knowledge doesn't cause her to go soft on anyone. The spiky hostility of "Mommy" is omni-directional. It is what "I shouldn't need to mention" that thrills us most in the main character description: we recognize that combination of pathos, willful self-deception, and cunning. Likewise, we recognize the impure, long-fermented alloy of intelligence, victimhood, and resentment in the speaker's voice. Then there is the disconcerting ventriloquial way in which the repeated "Mommy" phrases work—"Mommy tries to love, Mommy tries to get a job"—so that they seem to emanate from inside the Mommy-figure herself. It's not just that this poem breaks the primal commandment to Love Thy Mother; there's something visceral and invasive in the *manner* of the breaking. Brown's speaker operates aggressively with a fine-tuned knowingness about internalized sexism, American self-indulgence, and mother-child psychology. Only a very mean speaker could be so, so, so . . . *observant.*

Brown is unusual in contemporary poetry for her willingness to be thought ill of. In fact, it's significant that ugly-truth-tellers are much more common in our fiction than our poetry. Much of our mainstream poetry is constrained by an ethic of sincerity and the unstated wish to be admired (if not admired, liked; if not liked, sympathized with). American poetry still largely believes, as romantics have for a few hundred years, that a poem is straightforward autobiographical testimony to, among other things, the decency of the speaker. And, for all the freedom and "opening up" engendered by Confessionalism, to be uninhibitedly mean, we all know, is itself prohibited. Welcome to Poetry City: hurt someone's feelings—go to jail.

The problem with such civility is that it excludes all kinds of subject matter that cannot be handled without contamination of the handler. American poetry of the last few decades has specialized in empathy, and many extraordinary poems have been written in that spirit—but all that warmth has banished the cold eye of the prosecutor. To some extent, the decay of fierce analytical thinking in our poetry has been an outgrowth of the culture of Nice-ism.

It hasn't always been so. Once upon a time, Meanness was poetically permissible, even celebrated. Satire rejoices in the lampooning of human nature, in telling tales of vice and folly. Juvenal and Villon, Chaucer and Swift, Ben Jonson and Catullus—the poets of social satire slander their enemies, mock their neighbors, and tell tales on their lovers with glee. Spitting, punching below the belt, and face-slapping for them was a source of creative energy and pride. Here's the opening of Juvenal's "Satire II," still savagely fresh nineteen hundred years later:

> Northward beyond the Lapps to the world's end, the frozen
> Polar ice-cap—there's where I long to escape when I hear
> High-flown moral discourse from that clique in Rome who affect
> Ancestral peasant virtues as a front for their lechery.
> An ignorant crowd, too, for all the plaster busts
> Of Stoic philosophers on display in their houses:
> The nearest they come to doctrine is when they possess
> Some original portrait—Aristotle, or one of the Seven Sages—
> Hung on the library wall. Appearances are deceptive:

Every back street swarms with solemn-faced humbuggers.
You there—have you the nerve to thunder at vice, who are
The most notorious dyke among all our Socratic fairies?

But few, if any, want to get their hands dirty these days, and it costs us. Consider, just for example, the subject matter of race in America. Why haven't racial anxiety, shame, and hatred—such a large presence in American life—been more a theme in poetry by Caucasian Americans? The answer might be that empathy is profoundly inadequate as a strategy to some subjects. To really get at the subject of race, chances are, is going to require some unattractive, tricky self-expression, something adequate to the paradoxical complexities of privilege, shame, and resentment. To speak in a voice equal to reality in this case will mean the loss of observer-immunity status, will mean admitting that one is not on the sidelines of our racial realities, but actually in the tangled middle of them. Nobody is going to look good. Meanwhile, of course, American black poets have been putting the nasty topic on the table for a long time, in very personal ways.

In a wild, hilarious book, *Joker, Joker Deuce,* Paul Beatty, a young African American poet, explores the ins and outs of literary ethnicity with a savage kind of wit. Written in a hip-hop style, satire is a multi-use tool in Beatty's searching social surveys. What is exciting about Beatty's poems is not just their keen eye and considerable verbal dexterity, but the wide latitude of his targets. Yes, he definitely is an Angry Young Black Man, and yes, he likes to make fun of what he calls the "North American Whitey," but he is equally satirical about the complicated politics of Behaving Black. In his long poem "About the Author," for example, Beatty conflates and parodies American consumerism and the canonization of Martin Luther King:

but everybody's *talkin' bout a revolution*
including four fab white guys
in skinny ties
whose music nike used to sell tennis shoes pre-spike

just do it
you mean do it to it   no no that wont fly in iowa
if only martin luther king was still alive

      i can see it now   organ music   a choir
he'd be wearing red white and blue gym shoes sayin . . .

      this is mlk
      when im marchin on washington   *yes lord*
      coolin my heels in a birmingham jail
      backpedalin in memphis   *mmmmm hmmmn*
      running from german shepherds in selma
      cheatin on my wife in hattiesburg   *yes suh*

i thank god i wear air integrationists crossover trainers by nike

         hallelujah

In another section of the same long poem, the speaker satirizes his
own youthfully simplistic versions of racial injustice:

      we used to come home on college vacations
      pissed n miffed at the system

open the fridge

      there aint no kool-aid
      see mom how fucked up shit is

thats when sylvester come home
fresh out his yellow construction foreman pick-up truck
he'd dust the country music off his dungarees
reshape the chicago in his afro

look at the anger in our teary visined eyes
smell the hurt on our beer drenched breath
and say

revolutionary thrills
without revolutionary skills
will get you killed

the mud on my shoes
the arthritis on your mothers fingers
1000 hours of cosmetology school—
. . . .
nigga dont you see self hatred paid for your education

Meanness clears the air of sanctimony, falsehood, and denial, of our sentimental, ideological wishes about how things are alleged to be. Often, it recomplicates the issues. Because it does not intend to forgive nor ask forgiveness, because it does not imagine reconciliation as an end, meanness has an advantage over other kinds of discourse. Free of the complex accommodations required by "presenting a balanced view," or Being Fair-Minded, opinion can fly with original, sometimes unerring force.

At its most radical, meanness can even have the quality of metaphysical straight-talk. Some parables of Franz Kafka, certainly, and the stories of Flannery O'Connor, offer superb examples of metaphysical meanness. Czselaw Milosz also has written many poems that view humanity from a chilly altitude, with great clarity but little charity.

In the first two stanzas of Anna Akhmatova's poem "Twenty-first. Night," translated by Jane Kenyon, human affairs are seen from a great and weary distance. The poet directs a scornful, condescending gaze at the endless human preoccupation with romance:

Twenty-first. Night. Monday.
Silhouette of the capitol in darkness.
Some good-for-nothing—who knows why—
made up the tale that loves exists on earth.

People believe it, maybe from laziness
or boredom, and live accordingly:
they wait eagerly for meetings, fear parting,
and when they sing, they sing about love.

But the secret reveals itself to some
and on them, the silence settles down . . .
I found this out by accident
and now it seems I'm sick all the time.

Akhmatova is like the bad sister of the fairy godmother—she doesn't merely want us to know that love doesn't exist, that we've all been duped; she wants to emphasize that those who *do* believe in it are probably stupid and lazy, and that they belong to a long, generic tradition of stupid and lazy people. Her scathing, casually delivered pronouncement describes much of life, all of Reality TV, and whole chapters of anybody's personal history. Its cold authority is thrilling.

Thrilling, yes—but if the poem ended after two stanzas, it would seem narrow of heart. If the poetics of empathy can sometimes be simpleminded, satire also can be blind or petty, full of self-satisfaction without self-examination. The conclusion of Akhmatova's poem, which raises it to greatness, is the admission of her own sickness of spirit, her own romantic disappointment. The resonance of the poem becomes truly full when it admits a kind of empathy. But not, we might note, until the first two stanzas have enacted their stylish evisceration of the romantic, untainted by the whiff of memoir.

In poetry, as in life, meanness almost always has a personal flavor, and perhaps it is even more admirable for this lack of detachment. The mean speaker is not retired from the battles of selfhood, not removed to some philosophical resort where experience can be codified in tranquility. She or he is still down in the dirty human valley, fighting it out with the rest of us. In that way, the mean speaker may possess more convincing credentials than a kind or wise one.

In Akhmatova's fierce lyric complaint, a resonant vision has been distilled from the speaker's experience. It has been rendered clear and caustic, with wit and skill. But the part of the self that has died to get it has left its flavor behind, and, even in translation, the bitterness seeps through, sweetly vengeful, like a worm in the vodka.

TONY HOAGLAND (1953–2018) was the author of seven collections of poetry, including *Priest Turned Therapist Treats Fear of God* and *What Narcissism Means to Me*, a finalist for the National Book Critics Circle Award. He was also the author of four books of essays, including *The Art of Voice: Poetic Principles and Practice* and *Twenty Poems That Could Save America and Other Essays*. He received the Jackson Poetry Prize from Poets & Writers, the Mark Twain Award from the Poetry Foundation, and the O. B. Hardison Jr. Award from the Folger Shakespeare Library. Hoagland taught at the University of Houston and elsewhere, and lived in Santa Fe, New Mexico.

This book was designed by Rachel Holscher. It is set in 11/14 Warnock type by Prism Publishing Center, and manufactured by Bookmobile on acid-free, 100 percent postconsumer wastepaper.